"I commend Stacy Cline's spirit a [  ] writes sensitively, having experienced himself a deep confrontation with both horrific grief and healing grace. All humanity shares a common vulnerability to the impact of pain, death, human failure and demonic activity, and the bane of each wreaks havoc with the health, well-being and beauty God intends for us all. *Suffering Loss* will help many recover, offering readers practical counsel with biblical wisdom to discover 'beauty for ashes and the oil of joy for mourning.'"

JACK W. HAYFORD
*Chancellor, The King's Seminary; Founder, The Church On The Way*

"We had the privilege of walking with Stacy and Connie through this, the most traumatic experience of their lives. Because they have come through victoriously, this book can take you from grief to wholeness. The Clines have proven that, with the grace of God, grief is a process, not a destination. A must read for everyone struggling to see God's hand in difficult circumstances."

REV. PAUL JOHANSSON
*Chancellor, Elim Bible Institute*

"I have waited expectantly for this comfort to come, for this story to be told and for this teaching to be written—and it is my great privilege to recommend this book to anyone who is suffering or who seeks to help others through suffering of any kind. Having been one of those who has felt the pain of my friends, Stacy and Connie Cline, I have also believed for and witnessed the flow of grace to them and through them over the years since the trauma of loss hit their hearts and their home. From being with them as they laughed and loved together with their vibrant, expectant daughter, René, just days before her death to being with them as they staggered under the overwhelming load of sorrow, I am delighted to be with them in the celebration of redemption and restoration recorded in these pages. Here is the evidence that healing happens, that grace is given, that triumph can follow tragedy. This is more than a personal journal of a personal journey through grief. This is also a profoundly personal affirmation of the goodness of God. The traveler through sorrow in this story, the tested one, is also the teacher. As anyone who knows Stacy Cline would expect, he has grappled with issues while grounding us in the Word, keeping his tear-filled eyes 'looking unto Jesus.' Thus he has given us a spiritual guidebook that leads us all to refreshing fountains of Truth essential to the Christian soul—Truth that is in Jesus Christ our Lord alone."

REV. SYLVIA R. EVANS

*Founder/Director, Creative Word Ministries;*
*Faculty, Elim Bible Institute*

"If you have suffered deep loss in your life, this book will skillfully and tenderly direct your heart toward a path of healing. It will renew your confidence in God and His good purposes for your life."

BOB SORGE

*Author of* Pain, Perplexity & Promotion:
A Prophetic Interpretation Of The Book Of Job

"Many of us have been revived, renewed and restored as we embrace the lyrics of a special song, and often we discover that these words were birthed out of a painful season in the writer's life. In this very same way, I'm convinced that these words birthed out of pain from a shepherd, scholar, loving husband, father and friend will touch you to the core—and bring life and healing to your place of suffering."

REV. CHRIS BALL

*Senior Pastor, Lighthouse Community Fellowship;*
*General Secretary, Elim Fellowship*

"Those looking for quick and easy deliverance from distress, clear and certain answers to tough questions, and a story of happily-ever-after should go find another book. But if you suspect that life's deepest distresses are not so easily resolved, you will find in this book a soul mate discovering a road less traveled. *Suffering Loss* combines achingly honest memoir, deep pastoral compassion for all who hurt, and the eye of a teacher for bedrock theological principles that undergird the long and winding road leading from devastation to destiny."

DR. SHELDON SORGE
*Associate Director, The Louisville Institute*

"Stacy Cline is a wounded healer who in this book shares his story of heartbreaking loss and how he and his wife found a way through their pain. He has marked a trail of healing for you as only someone who has tasted suffering can do. These are not trite platitudes— these are pain-bought insights that will fill you with new hope. If you have tasted grief in any area of life, this book is for you."

REV. MIKE CAVANAUGH
*Vice-President, Elim Fellowship*

"Loss of any kind—especially that of a child, grandchild or spouse— can be the most debilitating experience for any of us in life. What Stacy shares with us from the very personal chapters of his family's sojourn is a journey from the abyss of suffocating despair, loss and emotional pain into a new world of hope, restored meaning and new-found purpose. Having the privilege of sharing these years together since their tragic loss, my family and I have deeply benefited from the depth of their restoration and healing and its continuing impact on the community of believers we both serve together. May everyone who reads their story benefit from the new life God's grace has brought to our dear friends and will no doubt bring to you as you embrace His loving purpose and grace in your own life."

REV. JEFF CLARK
*President, Elim Bible Institute*

"Opening up this book is like surgically opening up the human heart—one that beats robustly through death. How amazing is the transparent surrender of Stacy and Connie in this deeply private account of their lives—lives that weathered loss and actually succeed in answering the tough questions of trusting God, even with one's most precious treasures."

REV. NANCY CLARK
*President, Evangelical Women Leaders of the*
*National Association of Evangelicals;*
*Director, W.I.L.L.O.W. Women's Ministries, Elim Fellowship*

"In *Suffering Loss*, Stacy Cline weaves together the narrative of Scripture, the work of the comforter Spirit, and soul-searching reflection on his own personal tragedy to present us with a tapestry of trust in the promises of God. At the heart of this book is a theology of the Cross that confronts the well-intended but spiritually and emotionally crippling clichés common among Christians and the false expectations of North American Christians for a life of prosperity, ease and quick healing. The book resounds with the hope of healing and restoration for all those seeking God in the midst of suffering."

REV. THERESA F. LATINI, PH.D.
*Assistant Professor of Congregational and Community Care,*
*Luther Seminary*

# Suffering Loss

*Discovering the Blessing of Change, Growth, Healing & the Hope of a Beautiful Life*

STACY CLINE

FURROW
PRESS

*Suffering Loss:*
*Discovering the Blessing of Change, Growth, Healing & the Hope of a Beautiful Life*
Copyright © 2009 by Stacy Cline
Published by Furrow Press
P.O. Box 98
Big Flats, NY 14814-0098

The publishing style of Furrow Press capitalizes names and pronouns in Scripture and in this text that refer to the Godhead. Additionally, certain words of Christian significance are capitalized also (e.g., Kingdom, Bible, the Cross, Scripture, etc.).

Edited by Edie Mourey (www.furrowpress.com)

Cover and interior design by David G. Danglis / Pinwheel Creative
Cover photos: dchadwick & Jason_V, www.iStockphoto.com

Printed in the United States of America
Library of Congress Control Number: 2009939715
International Standard Book Number: 978-0-9800196-3-6

# DEDICATION

*This book is presented as an offering to the King of my life.*
*It is my deepest prayer that its contents will bring honor to Him.*

# CONTENTS

# ACKNOWLEDGMENTS

One of the great joys of writing my first book is the opportunity I now have to say thank you to the special people who have made it possible. There are many I must mention!

I begin first with my wife and best friend, Connie, who has experienced every pain with me in the process of birthing the life principles in this book. René and Jessica were our girls. We have shared horrendous loss and walked through the darkness together. We have clung to one another when we were out of our minds with grief and have emerged on the other side of anguish still deeply in love with Jesus and one another. Thank you, baby.

Deep appreciation also goes to my youngest daughter, Danielle. You have always been my "special, made-to-order" girl, the daughter I prayed for. I place high value on the friendship that has developed between us as we have walked through grief together. You are my daughter, friend and confidant—a priceless treasure. I love and cherish you, sweetheart.

How can we say thank you to you, Doug? You were never a son-in-law but always the true son of our hearts. No one could have been a better husband to our René. You were the husband we prayed for when she was a baby, and your love was truly the fulfillment of many of her deepest dreams. You honored her memory with the greatest integrity in the way that you grieved for her, and Mom and I are forever grateful. Your continued love and openness of heart have brought the blessings of a new daughter and grandchildren into our lives. You are a man of honor, son, and we love you more than words can express.

To Michelle, you are the astonishing gift of grace we now count as our "middle" daughter. You walked into our hearts the moment that we first met you and became a "daughter of destiny" to us. It would be impossible to measure the joy that you have brought into our lives, and we love you as a true daughter that would have come from Connie's own body. Your reciprocating love to Mom, Danielle and me is a miracle of grace and healing, and you are loved and cherished in every way.

Thanks as well to our incredible grandchildren: Katherine, Daniel, Anna Joy and David. As we have shared on numerous occasions, you have brought deep healing to our hearts. The last part of this book never would have been written without the love you have freely given to Grandma and me. Each one of you has brought great joy to us with your unconditional and unreserved love. You have been channels of blessing, and we hold you all in our hearts with the deepest love and affection possible.

I also want to especially thank our dear friends, Don and Mary Sandwell. Your commitment and loyalty to Connie and me provided us with an anchor in our walk of grief. You are greatly loved and respected. You never for a moment sought to exclude us from the formation of Doug's new family. Connie and I will never be able to thank you enough for the inclusive love that has flowed continually and freely from your hearts to ours.

To my friend, Chris Ball, you have been a "friend that sticks closer than a brother" and walked with me for years in the deepest trenches of my pain. I will never forget how you stood with me in the bedroom as I was packing to fly to the funeral. I was so overwhelmed with pain that I was unable to put my clothes in the suitcase. You lovingly packed my stuff for me as I sat on the edge of the bed debilitated with emotional shock and anguish. You are appreciated and greatly loved.

Deep thanks also go to our dear friends, Chris and Pauline Pedersen. Calling you on our Black Friday was one of the hardest calls because we knew what the awful announcement would do to your hearts. You were always a second mom and dad to our girls—and your home was a spiritual hospital in the early years of our pain. We made our way south as wounded and bleeding warriors, and you never made us feel like we were a burden. We found love, comfort and healing in the peaceful sanctuary of your home. You are always in our hearts with profound gratitude and deepest love.

Thanks as well to our friend and colleague, Sylvia Evans. Although you were unable to attend the funeral, you dramatically rearranged your schedule to be with us within hours of the funeral's conclusion. You sat for hours (literally) with our whole family and ministered grace. Unlike Job's comforters, your imparted principles of wisdom laid a foundation that we have built on to the present day. Thanks also for the many hours you spent with the manuscript in its final stages. Your suggestions were invaluable. We love you so very much and will always be grateful.

I extend special heartfelt thanks to all of our colleagues at Elim. You walked with us in our ongoing ministry together, and we strongly felt your love and support. Paul and Gloria Johansson deserve special mention. The flowers and cards that would arrive years later on the anniversary of René's death were so deeply comforting. You held us in your heart and let us know that you would never forget our girls. You have been true friends and our greatest mentors in life and ministry. We love you and will always be grateful.

To our colleagues, Harry and Connie Vellekoop, I offer our heartfelt thanks and love. Well into our second year of grief, we discovered that you were not only holding us in your hearts, but also praying for us every single day. We will never know this side of eternity the impact of those prayers, but they are a part of our healing, and we are deeply grateful.

Special thanks go to Brick Cliff of W.I.N. Ministries. Your friendship, practical help and investment in the book made it a reality as we jumped over final hurdles on our way to the finish line. Thanks for gently but firmly "getting up in my face." It was a great honor to film the teaching of the book with W.I.N. Ministries, and I pray that the DVD will be used by the Lord to touch people in many nations.

I will always cherish the words of my friend, Sheldon Sorge, who wrote such a precious foreword to this book. Although years and miles have separated us, my dear brother, the bond of love and respect is still as strong as ever.

Thankfully, I feel no allegiance to the pompous rules of academia that discourage expressing gratitude to a writer's editor—so a special thanks to Edie Veach Mourey who worked so hard with me on the manuscript. Your prayerful, patient, encouraging and razorsharp editing produced an end result I would never have achieved on my own. What began as a business arrangement ended in a friendship.

I also want to express gratitude to my friend, Dave Danglis, and Pinwheel Creative for your work and design layout. Your gift and skill brought the necessary finishing touches to the project.

Finally, a sincere thanks to all of my colleagues and other leaders who gave such kind endorsements for this book. I felt humbled and empowered by the imparted blessings of your words.

# FOREWORD

René Cline was my eldest daughter's first childhood friend. Three or four years older than Sonya, René was to her the epitome of grace, wisdom and beauty; she wanted to be just like René. Fast forward twenty years, and the unthinkable happens. This beautiful young lady who will ever live in our imaginations as the perfect ideal to which girls could aspire is snatched suddenly from this life by a terrible tragedy. How could a merciful God permit such a senseless suspension of a beautiful, God-consecrated life?

I hadn't seen René and her family over that twenty-year span, as our lives took very different paths. Still, the news of René's untimely death doubled me over in disbelieving anguish. How much more would it devastate her family? I could scarcely imagine.

This book will take us on an odyssey as treacherous as anyone can be made to navigate. It leads us from unspeakable loss and unquenchable agony to unshakable trust in God's ultimate goodness. Those looking for quick and easy deliverance from distress, clear and certain answers to tough questions, and a story of happily-ever-after should go find another book. But if you suspect that life's deepest distresses are not so easily resolved, you will find in this book a soul mate discovering a road less traveled, a journey to new life and blessing that seemed impossible to imagine for many years.

*Suffering Loss* combines achingly honest memoir, deep pastoral compassion for all who hurt and the eye of a teacher for bedrock theological principles that undergird the long and winding road leading from devastation to destiny. Stacy anchors us firmly from sliding down either of two slippery slopes that cause us to miss what God would do in us through the experience of loss and pain. On the one hand, he exposes both the inadequacy and the unfaithfulness of the teaching that loss and pain cannot be God's will for us, and therefore they should lead us to discover and repair defects in our faith. On the other hand, Stacy does not permit us simply to capitulate to the suffering, as though God is just as overcome and stymied by it as we are. Slicing through the knot in the middle of these frayed falsehoods, he leads fellow sufferers to embrace both the mystery *and* the trustworthiness of God's good providence.

More is at stake, however, than understanding and accepting the suffering that God has permitted us to endure. Stacy shows powerfully how our own suffering can produce springs of comfort and encouragement for others, as we yield our distresses to the source of all comfort.

*There is no sugarcoating here of the depth of human pain.* In fact, the deeper the pain, the greater the comfort we need and, therefore, the greater accumulated storehouse of comfort that we can extend to others.

Incomprehensible suffering, as awful as it truly is, need not be the final word; from the throes of our death God can and does raise up new life for others. Stacy's testimony to how this has emerged for him and his family beautifully demonstrates this power of God at work, and invites all who have suffered to embrace the fullness of blessing that can come only through sharing with others the comfort that we have received in our own dark valleys. Both the comfort we receive and the comfort we are privileged thereby to share ultimately come from the hand of a God who—through loss as well as gain, through pain as well as pleasure—loves us more than we can possibly imagine.

Dr. Sheldon W. Sorge
*Associate Director, The Louisville Institute*
*October 2009*

# PREFACE

Loss pierces our lives—loss of every type and shadow—the loss of a marriage through divorce, the death of a loved one, the loss of a job. The daily struggle with a debilitating physical illness and the agony of praying for a wayward child or a loved one who is resisting help or intervention can all thrust the sharp blade of grief into our souls.

Yes, even believers experience such loss. The Body of Christ has members who have suffered the traumatic pain of physical, emotional, sexual and spiritual abuse. These cry out today for spiritual healing. Those of us who have experienced loss in its varied forms can never achieve our maximum potential in life *or* ministry until we have been healed in our hearts.

The Church has been inundated with preaching and teaching that seeks to empower believers to receive and experience the blessing of God. Usually, this blessing has been defined in the context of abundant finances and material possessions. Any material deficit or personal struggle in an individual's life has often been construed as evidence of a lack of faith on his or her part.

The same perspective has also been applied to human suffering, physical infirmities and emotional pain. Some purport that, if our faith is strong enough, then we will not experience illness, certainly not terminal illness, and our lives will be free from pain and suffering. But is that really the truth? What does the Bible actually teach us about loss? Can suffering and catastrophic loss be experienced within the good, acceptable and perfect will of God? What life principles did our Lord and the New Testament church model regarding suffering?

I want to address some of these real-life questions within the pages of this book you now hold in your hands. I desire to impart encouragement, comfort and healing to hurting hearts by identifying specific principles I see in Scripture and have seen effective in my life and in the lives of others.

The need for these truths has become clear to me as I have watched Christians flounder in times of personal pain. Many precious people have encountered spiritual shipwreck as they have sought desperately to reconcile the Bible and personal suffering with the unbalanced teaching given by some spiritual leaders, implying that suffering is a sign of something out of order in their spiritual lives.

Born out of intense pain and grief in my own life, the message I share with you in this book is written prayerfully and humbly as a new response to this question: What does it mean to be truly blessed by God?

It's also my conviction that the principles presented here can provide an understanding of how growth and fruitfulness occur during periods of suffering and loss in the believer's life. You will be challenged to see that God is looking for certain heart attitudes that are instrumental in releasing growth, fruitfulness and blessing into our lives. As we begin our journey together in quest for this blessing, it's my prayer that the Holy Spirit will lead us into His truth that always sets us free.

Stacy Cline
*October 2009*

# CHAPTER 1

# Black Friday

It was an unusually cold and snowy Friday evening in early March, the kind of miserable spring weather that made me wish my home was in southern Florida. My wife, Connie, and I were making ourselves comfortable in the hotel room where we would be spending the night. We had been invited to facilitate a marriage seminar for a church in Syracuse, New York, and the first teaching session was the next morning.

After checking in, I left Connie in the room and went to forage for supplies, returning with our normal hotel meal of Coke, pizza and wings—a supper for true champions.

My wife had spread out notes and Bible on one of the beds and was preparing her heart for the ministry of the next day. I loaded my plate with the appointed rations and settled on the other bed to see how my favorite basketball team was faring in the Big East tournament. I became completely engrossed in the game, watching with excitement as my Syracuse Orangemen jumped out to an early lead.

"That's all right, sweetheart. I'll do the praying for both of us," my wife said playfully.

Understanding that her DNA completely lacked the "March Madness" gene, I nodded enthusiastically, attempting to look especially pious and anointed while munching my wings.

The sound of Connie's voice reminded me how deeply I loved my family. We had just experienced a wonderful family reunion made complete by a visit from our oldest married daughter, René. She had flown north from her home in Virginia Beach to spend an entire week with Mom, Dad, sister Danielle and other friends. René was five months pregnant and especially excited to receive all the beautiful maternity clothes lovingly made by her devoted mother.

Our reunion week was filled with extra excitement as we watched the sonogram video that revealed a girl in our daughter's womb. She and her husband, Doug (a true son of our heart), had already named their tiny unborn daughter, Jessica Grace. I almost wore out my video player, watching over and over again the image of our precious baby granddaughter sucking her thumb.

The night before René returned home, our family time culminated with a special twenty-fourth birthday dinner for her. Although we cried as we said good-bye at the airport, our sadness was tempered with joy knowing we would see each other soon for Easter. A regular week of full ministry followed for Connie and me, and eight days later we were in Syracuse for the seminar.

As I lay on the bed, my heart was overflowing with gratitude for how graciously God had blessed our family. It seemed hard to fathom that the babies we had brought home from the hospital just a "few" years before had grown so quickly into beautiful young women. After completing high school, they had each chosen to attend Elim Bible Institute where I was dean and teacher.

After finishing Elim's three-year program, René had expressed the desire to marry her college sweetheart. I was honored beyond words when she came to me and said, "Dad, there is no minister that I respect more than you, so I want you to walk me down the aisle, give me away and then perform the ceremony."

Our family joyously gave our full blessing because Doug was the man that we had prayed for; he was suited ideally to be our daughter's covenant partner for life.

It was two years after they were married that they decided the time was right for them to expand their family. With only four months left in René's pregnancy, we were experiencing the thrilling expectation of our first grandchild.

*It just doesn't get any better than this,* I thought, but suddenly it did. One of the Syracuse forwards slam-dunked the basketball, shaking the backboard and bringing the Madison Square Garden crowd to its feet. All of this blessing in my family *and* a Syracuse win in the Big East quarterfinal game? *It really is just too good to be true.*

The harsh, loud ring of the hotel phone jolted me back to reality. "It's probably the senior pastor checking in with us," I said to Connie.

The voice on the other end, however, was not that of a church leader. It was the voice of my 21-year-old daughter, Danielle, and her inflection as she spoke the word, "Dad," made my blood run cold.

"Sweetheart, what's the matter?" I asked.

Her voice trembled and wavered as she responded, "Doug just called and said that René has had an allergic reaction. She's been rushed to the hospital, Dad, and Doug says that it's serious."

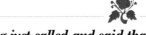

*"Doug just called and said that René has had an allergic reaction. She's been rushed to the hospital, Dad, and Doug says that it's serious."*

We talked for a moment, trying to secure more details, but the initial statement contained all the available facts: René had been taken to the hospital emergency room. After establishing that Doug had our hotel phone number, I articulated a simple plan.

"Okay, honey, this is what we're going to do. We'll stay close to the phone and begin to pray."

As I hung up the handset to tell my wife the news, I noticed the clock. It was 8:10 p.m.

Connie and I immediately went on our faces before the Lord. As we began to pray, my mind was racing to process the information that I had. René and Doug had been attending a large banquet at the Christian university where they were students. I knew that about 800 believers would have been in attendance. *That's good,* I thought. *It means that my girl had immediate prayer.*

In recent years, René had suffered with several allergic reactions of varying intensity. Her physician had prescribed an EpiPen autoin-jector that she always carried with her, so I began to feel positive about the situation. She was receiving prayer, she would have had her shot, and she was at the hospital getting medical attention.

"I'm sure she's okay," I said hopefully. But as I continued to pray, I reflected on Doug's personality. Our son-in-law was the perfect description of a tender warrior. He could be so gentle, and yet he was a tower of strength and, most significantly, a man who *never* exag-gerated. If Doug said it was serious, there was cause for alarm. I had to stop my thoughts from going further.

From my knees, I gave a sidelong glance at the clock. It seemed as though we had been praying for hours. Only 45 minutes had passed.

As my prayer intensified, I continued to fight the battle between faith and anxiety. My thoughts raced backwards 19 years to another medical crisis in our family. Our daughter, Danielle, a toddler at the time, had defied the security of a childproof bottle and had taken several strong prescription pills meant to neutralize my summer allergies. The ambulance trip to the hospital had been the begin-ning of an all-night vigil in which her life had hung in the balance. That night had coincided with a life lesson the Holy Spirit had been teaching me in the area of trust.

In a study of the book of Daniel, I had marveled at the three young Hebrew men who were cast into Nebuchadnezzar's fire because they refused to bow to the king's image. In Daniel 3:17-18, they confidently said: "'The God we serve is able to save us . . . and He will rescue us from your hand.'" And then they added this aston-ishing footnote: "'. . . but, even if He does not . . . we will not serve your gods.'"

As I had followed the ambulance in my car, I had become aware of how dramatically that "trust" principle applied to the life of my two-year-old daughter. In reflecting on this distant but vivid memory, I recalled how God had come to my heart at midnight and asked the following question: "Son, are you willing to trust me even if she dies?"

With tears in my eyes, I had touched the body of our little girl, still in her diaper, and said, "Jesus, she belongs to You. If You want her, she's Yours."

God was merciful, and five hours later Danielle had come out of her coma singing, "Jesus loves me this I know." She was healed by the Lord's power, and never experienced any side effects.

I brought these memories into the present as the clock showed 9:05 p.m.

*Okay,* I thought, *I've been in this situation before. This is another advanced lesson in trust and must be what Abraham felt as he took Isaac to Mount Moriah.*

Mount Moriah was the place where the Lord tested Abraham and later promised rich blessing because he had not withheld his son (Genesis 22:1, 16-17).

*God must be testing my heart again in the same way. If I respond correctly, I'll receive my daughter back from the altar just as I did 19 years ago.*

I cried from the depth of my spirit, "Jesus, I love You with all of my heart. Please touch René and Jessica and deliver their lives from this crisis. I trust You to act powerfully and give life." My prayers were joined together with the intercession of my wife in a stereo chorus that rose to the Father as the minutes crawled by.

Suddenly, the phone rang, piercing the air like a siren. It was 9:15 p.m., and my hand trembled uncontrollably as I reached to answer.

Doug was sobbing on the line, and my body felt the tremor of cold chills with the realization that there would be no miracle for our family on this Friday evening.

"Dad," he cried, "there's no way to soften this. We've lost our girls."

The moan released from my soul communicated the awful truth to my wife, and I saw her contract into the fetal position. As Doug and I cried together, he described as best he could the horrific events that had unfolded.

René had experienced a condition known as anaphylactic shock after eating her fish entrée at the banquet. The EpiPen autoinjector had been in her purse, and Doug had administered two shots of epinephrine. He had taken her to a side exit for fresh air and then had quickly driven her to the medical center almost across the street.

At the banquet, the master of ceremonies had interrupted the program schedule to call everyone to prayer as the medical team labored to save our daughter and granddaughter. All spiritual and medical efforts were to no avail, and the Lord received our girls into His presence.

After communicating that we would be on the first available flight to Virginia Beach, I hung up and looked at my wife on the bed. I was confronted with an image that I pray I never have to see again: Connie's body had retracted into a writhing ball, as she cried over and over—"Not my girl, not my girl, not my girl." I pulled her into my arms as we uttered together the moan of anguish that can never be explained but is understood by those who have felt the sharp blade of grief as it eviscerates the soul.

The moments and hours that followed were utterly surreal. Calling Danielle was the first painful phone call, followed by others to our parents and friends who needed to know. Every call was different and yet the same—each person expressing shock and disbelief, forcing me to repeat the *death* word a second time. No one could believe the news.

*"Four days later, we buried our beautiful 24-year-old daughter with our perfectly formed granddaughter in her arms."*

Four days later, we buried our beautiful 24-year-old daughter with our perfectly formed granddaughter in her arms. The pain we experienced in the days leading up to the funeral was debilitating, yet simultaneously infused with the undergirding grace of God.

Doug and René had been deeply involved in their local church, and their cell group came around our family like a wall, expressing Christ's love and embracing us with "pillows of comfort" as they helped us in countless practical ways. I was reminded moment by moment that we were a part of the Body of Christ.

One of the many memories etched in my soul from this nightmare period was the task of purchasing the dress in which we would bury our little granddaughter, Jessica. Going to a store to shop for that garment loomed as an impossible hurdle to the whole family. Then Cheryl and Coleen, two young mothers from the cell group, presented us with several infant dresses that they had lovingly purchased for our approval, and we wept uncontrollably as we made our choice. These two "angels of mercy" had profoundly touched us as Christ's Body.

We also were faced with the necessity of picking out a casket for our girls. As we walked into the display room, Doug almost collapsed under the emotional weight of the choice we were being forced to make. Coffins made of wood, metal, satin, brass, gold, silver and platinum.

*I don't want any of them!* I inwardly screamed. The funeral director tried to sell us the most expensive model with the suggestion that the body of our daughter would be "preserved forever."

*What am I doing here looking at coffins for two unfinished lives?* I felt like shrieking in agony as my emotions were stretched to the breaking point. I wanted to punch the exploitative funeral director in the face, but at a deeper level, I wanted to hit God while screaming, "No, no, no!" My hands remained at my sides, however, as God's grace enabled me to take the next step.

The morning of the funeral arrived. I chose to travel to the funeral home with Doug and his dad because we wanted to pay our last private respects to our girls.

After we arrived at the funeral home, the three of us stood close to one another as each individually approached the casket. I stood and stared at my beautiful granddaughter, Jessica, whom I would never hold in this life. I touched René's long blonde hair, shaking my head in disbelief and denial. It had been just eleven days ago that I sat with her at the airport, listening to all the exciting dreams she shared for her future. I wouldn't have believed it possible to feel greater pain than I did at that moment as I stood remembering, but then I watched Doug approach the casket. I witnessed his intense brokenness as he sobbed and then wiped away his tears with my daughter's hair. The moment was dreadful and yet somehow sacred as a personal Calvary was enacted in my soul. I felt as though I needed supernatural power just to take my next breath and certainly my next steps—steps I'd have to take as I walked away from the casket to return to my family and bring them to the funeral.

Many friends and family from far and near surrounded us as our family came into the overflowing sanctuary where we would worship through tears and celebrate hope. Through many eulogies, we heard how our daughter's young life had touched many people, especially children, and had glorified her Lord, which was always her heart's desire.

After the funeral, we proceeded to the cemetery for the interment service. I was faced with the final, awful step—that of looking into the cold hole in which the bodies of our girls would be placed. The knowledge that René and Jessica were with Jesus and that we would be united together in the Eternal Kingdom seemed to bring little comfort at the moment. I had always thought the death of a child must be the most awful pain a parent could be asked to endure. As I walked away from the cemetery on that sunny Virginia day, staggering under the agony filling my whole being, I sensed I had been right. I understood intuitively that I was moving into the darkest night of my soul.

In Psalm 23:4, David declares, "Even though I walk through the valley of the shadow of death, I will fear no evil, for You are with Me." Traditionally, we have understood that verse to describe the comforting presence of the Lord when we encounter the appointed time of our personal death, and it is true that Jesus will be with us to impart special grace as we cross the threshold into eternity.

In the process of grief, however, my family and I have learned there are many different kinds of "death shadows" and corresponding valleys that we are called to walk through. I have come to understand "grief is the shadow of the love it reflects," as our friend, Sylvia Evans, shared with us just after the funeral. If grief is actually the shadow of the love we had for the one who was lost, then we can say that the *deeper* the love, the *longer* the shadow. "It's not the duration of that love, but its depth, its intensity and its intimacy that determines the length of its shadow," she explained, "until the light of divine comfort comes and drives the shadows away."

*"If grief is actually the shadow of the love we had for the one who was lost, then we can say that the* **deeper** *the love, the* **longer** *the shadow."*

In the immediate aftermath of the funeral, we received some valuable insights from people who understood grief. We remember well, however, some of the so-called truths that were not so helpful. Some told me that God loved my daughter so much He had received her prematurely into His presence. Aside from the theological problems I had with that statement, I had to wonder what it said about our family who was left behind, *Didn't God love us deeply as well, and if so how could He allow this to happen?*

Two weeks after the funeral, I found myself sitting in one of our campus chapel services. People were very involved in the worship time, expressing joy, dancing, shouting and clapping as they sang praises to the Lord. I was so overcome with my pain that I sat down and reverently bowed my head. I had neither desire nor ability to enter into the joyous explosion of worship taking place all around me. I didn't feel like joyfully shouting; I wanted instead to fall to the carpet and cry in the agony of my pain.

As I struggled with this inner conflict, trying as best I could to express my love to Christ, I felt the hand of one of my students on my shoulder. "You must demonstrate the victory of the Lord to the students in an observable way," the woman whispered in my ear. I didn't know what to say in response.

As time went on, others challenged us with the strong exhortation, "It's been several months now. You must get on with your life." Still other people sought to bring encouragement and perspective by saying that the first year would be the hardest. I hoped in my heart they were right, but I discovered instead that they were not. In fact, as my family walked "through the valley of the shadow of death," our pain intensified in the second year, with the third year being almost unbearable.

My wife and I agree now that a significant corner was finally turned in the midpoint of our fourth year. The deep waves of grief flooding my body, soul and spirit caused me to cry out with David— "How long must I wrestle with my thoughts and every day have sorrow in my heart?" (Psalm 13:2). Then a hopeful thought began to work its way into the wrestling process: *Would it be possible to grow spiritually and bear fruit in the experience of this kind of pain and loss?*

At the time of my writing this book, 13 years have passed since my daughter and granddaughter died. Now, I want to tell the rest of the story, answering my own question and describing how spiritual growth and fruit-bearing actually occurred in the life of my family.

It has been a long, arduous journey, and many times it seemed we would never experience any substantial healing and growth in the process. But it *has* happened, and we can now see that, through our walk of grief, the Holy Spirit imparted several biblical principles into the very core of our lives. These are the life principles I desire to share in the pages that follow. These six biblical principles describe the possibility of healing and fruitfulness when confronted with the reality of suffering, grief and loss. Although I will be speaking from the context of losing my daughter and granddaughter, I believe that these principles will have application to a broader experience of human suffering. I pray they will help you, whatever the depth of your grief or the nature of your suffering. Let us go now to the first principle that I want to share.

# CHAPTER 2

# The Grip of Confusion

## *Principle 1:*
### *Healing and growth are experienced when we trust God with our why questions.*

The birth of my children produced nothing less than a profound revolution in my daily experience with God. When I became a father at 23 years of age, I had been living in a committed relationship with Jesus for about five years. As I reflect on my journey during those early years, I can clearly see the patterns of spiritual growth the apostle John describes in his first epistle (1 John 2:12-14).

## LEVELS OF SPIRITUAL GROWTH

In verse 12, John says, "I write to you, dear children, because your sins have been forgiven on account of His name." This is where it begins for all who enter God's Kingdom. Experiencing complete forgiveness brings incredible joy and releases a jolt of spiritual adrenaline that makes us ready to walk on water. The supernatural cleansing is imparted to us because we have placed our faith in the finished work of the Cross, and it becomes the cornerstone for all our continued spiritual growth. After conversion, I walked in the exhilaration of forgiveness as one of God's "dear children" and became desirous of introducing everyone I encountered to the Savior who had made this mercy available to me.

As I continued to grow in my walk with Christ, I discovered the defining characteristics of a "young man." John says, "I write to you, young men, because you are strong, and the Word of God lives in you . . ." (1 John 2:14). The Bible became the most important book in the world to me, and I constantly studied it. When the prophet Jeremiah declared, "Your words came" and "I ate them" and "they were my joy and my heart's delight" (Jeremiah 15:16), I knew exactly what he meant. I was so consumed with my desire to study the Scriptures that I enrolled as a full-time student in Bible school. The reality of personal forgiveness coupled with the study of God's living Word began to define my whole existence.

And then I discovered the Devil. The growing awareness of demonic resistance and the call to spiritual warfare did not come as a fearful or disturbing revelation to me. After all, I was a "young man," and John addresses this level of growth by saying: "I write to you, young men, because you are strong, and the Word of God lives in you, and you have overcome the evil one" (14). What demonic force could stand in the way of a forgiven warrior who was full of the living Word of God? I was afraid of nothing and moved with reckless faith into spiritual situations that would have made most angels tremble. The Devil was just another mountain to climb and conquer as I found myself proclaiming with the 72 ministering disciples— "'Lord, even the demons submit to us in Your name'" (Luke 10:17).

There was, however, a missing piece in my spiritual growth pattern because I lacked an intimate relationship with God, the Father, who had imparted His forgiveness and power. In the middle of John's teaching on the levels of spiritual growth, he describes the children as "having known the Father."

In biblical salvation, we come face-to-face not only with God's *provision*, but also with His *Person*. Jesus tells us that knowing the Father is the foundation and focus of eternal life—"'Now this is eternal life: that they may know You, the only true God, and Jesus Christ, whom You have sent'" (John 17:3).

In my early encounter with Jesus, I had begun to know the Father as a new member of His family, but I was to discover that John is calling me forward into a deeper level of intimacy and maturity when he says, "I write to you fathers, because you have known Him who is from the beginning" (1 John 2:13). With these words, the apostle challenges each believer with a life principle that never changes: The essence of true Christian maturity is always measured by the depth of our relationship with Father God.

This fundamental truth confronts a core belief of our results-oriented, contemporary Christian culture, where success in ministry and life are measured by the spiritual exploits that have been performed in the name of Jesus. How many demons have been cast out? How many miracles and healings

*"The essence of true Christian maturity is always measured by the depth of our relationship with Father God."*

have been performed? How large is our church, and what percentage of growth has been experienced in the past year?

We seem to have forgotten about the many who will say to Jesus on the final day of accountability—"'Lord, Lord, did we not prophesy in Your name, and in Your name drive out demons and perform many miracles?' Then I will tell them plainly, 'I never knew you. Away from Me, you evildoers!'" (Matthew 7:22-23). In the end, Jesus will be looking for *relationship*, not *results*; He will not be looking primarily for how well we have performed spiritual activities.

God in His faithfulness revealed the presence of this relational deficiency in my own life as a young man. I needed to mature into fatherhood and understand the Father heart of God—and this revelation began with the experience of bringing my first newborn daughter home from the hospital.

## INTIMACY AND TRUST

I will never forget the wonderful day we brought René home. She was born in 1972, a time when fathers were traditionally shut out of the birthing process. I had even been forced to stand in the hall when our baby was brought into the room at feeding time, and I had not been allowed to hold her. The only visual contact I experienced with my new daughter was staring at her through the Plexiglas window of the hospital nursery.

The morning of Connie's discharge from the maternity ward was a day never to be forgotten. We returned home to our little apartment, and after I positioned myself in the rocking chair, my daughter was laid into my arms for the first time. I lifted the pink receiving blanket to count her little fingers and toes, and I began to cry as I dedicated her to the Lord. My heart felt ready to burst with joy and gratitude as I gently held our little eight-pound miracle close to my chest. Little did I understand the profound life lessons that the Lord would teach me through the experience of becoming a father to our firstborn and the daughters who would follow.

I immediately began to realize the implications of praying, "Our Father, who art in heaven...." I was amazed that God's love for me was being reflected in the relationship that I shared with my girls. Not only was I concerned about all the details of their futures, but I also knew I would never make a deliberate decision that did not have their best interests at heart.

As an imperfect father, I made more than my share of mistakes in parenting, but never would I have made an intentional or a malicious decision to hurt or injure my girls. This understanding began to change my relationship with Father God, and I began to trust Him more deeply and completely.

I knew then (and know now) how unconditional His love was for me and how perfectly He was watching over all the many facets of my life. God wanted intimacy with me as intensely as I wanted to share a love relationship with my daughters. I was discovering the deeper dimensions of spiritual growth that John describes in his epistle, and my relationship with Father grew stronger because of all He was teaching me through my children. *I can rest completely in His watchful care over my life,* I began to think.

Many times in my pastoral teaching I would hear myself say to students: "When you come to Father God, you enter into relationship with One who will never hurt you or injure you." I believed this with all of my heart, and I had learned this from my parenting.

## A HARSH REALITY

On March 8, 1996, all the spiritual foundations of my relationship with Father were shaken as I struggled in my grief to understand what had happened to our family. The laser focus of my pain went directly to God because the *if only* questions had been dramatically eliminated. I wasn't able to say, "If only my daughter had received the prayers of other Christians," or, "If only she had received emergency medical attention." Our daughter had been provided with immediate medical care in her crisis and was attending a banquet where 800 believers had interceded for her life.

In my anguish, I was brought face-to-face with my heavenly Father as the *why* questions poured out of my soul. My daughter was a loving worshiper with God's call on her life. As I added two plus two on my spiritual calculator, it was coming out five as I cried, "Lord, how could this possibly be allowed in Your sovereign plan?"

Months after her death, I lovingly held René's *Study Bible* as I examined passages she had marked with different colors and notes. The Bible reflected her love of color, and the pages at times gave off the appearance of a rainbow. As I looked more closely, I was able to determine her personal coded system, highlighting the passages closest to her heart with the color purple. I wept as I came to Psalm 121 where every verse was marked with that special color: "He who watches over you will not slumber . . . the Lord will keep you from all harm—He will watch over your life" (121:3, 7).

I tried to reconcile the certainty of my loss with God's clear promise to provide safety and protection, but His Word seemed to taunt me in my pain. The harsh reality of my agony was challenging the very lessons that God had taught me through fatherhood.

## JOB'S COMFORTERS

Certain well-meaning brothers and sisters tried repeatedly to answer my spiritual questions by imparting the pseudo-wisdom of empty clichés. I now realize that people who have not experienced deep loss in their own lives will be especially uncomfortable when they encounter pain in others. They desire to jump in and fix the hurt by using superficial "band-aids" to bind major wounds. In the early days of our grief walk, we were confronted with many of these non-biblical clichés.

*"I now realize that people who have not experienced deep loss in their own lives will be especially uncomfortable when they encounter pain in others."*

Some suggested that our girls had died because of a lack of faith in the intercession process. These claimed that, if people had been truly "praying in faith," their deaths would never have occurred because it's *always* God's will to heal. Others suggested that their deaths were related to judgment and an unbroken "generational curse" working in our family. Another bold suggestion was that Satan was responsible for our daughter's death, "sneaking" in to work his evil in an unguarded moment.

All of these proposed answers fundamentally broke down at two levels. First of all, such answers poured more pain into hearts that were already broken. It was nothing less than emotional cruelty to suggest that a person's lack of faith was responsible for the death of a loved one, or that a horrible tragedy was related to sin in his or her life. These were the very suggestions that were thrown at Job as he suffered with the accusations of his friends during the devastating shaking that God allowed in his life.

The second reason these easy answers failed was that they reflected a defective, unbiblical theology. It could be argued that all of Job's losses came at the hand of Satan, but to hold the Devil ultimately accountable for Job's pain is to miss the truth of the story. The

Devil had consistently failed in his attempts to attack Job because God had extended protection to him and his family. We can almost hear the exasperation in the Enemy's voice as he declares: "'Have You not put a hedge around him and his household and everything he has?'" (Job 1:10).

Can it be stated anymore clearly than that? Satan had no access to God's servant because the protective hedge covered every part of Job's life. In a very real sense, Job was invincible spiritually because the Lord watched over him daily. One of the themes that emerge from this story is this: *The High King of the universe makes a sovereign choice to remove a portion of the protective "hedge."*

At the end of the book when the Lord speaks out of the whirlwind, Satan is never mentioned because God takes full responsibility for what has happened in the life of His son, Job. If God is *able* to prevent something but chooses instead to *allow* it, then we are brought face-to-face with the King of kings.

In my personal grief and pain, I felt as if I were left alone with God to wrestle with the *why* questions. The *what if* questions had been negated by circumstances, and the *faith, sin and Satan* questions were eliminated by Scripture.

Like Job, I was having the awesome experience of encountering God in the whirlwind as I shouted out the protest of my *whys*—why didn't God intervene for a young woman who loved Him so much? Why would her destiny be cut short and her life left unfinished? Why was God silent when my life had been shattered? How could I reconcile the love of my heavenly Father with the harsh reality of my unspeakable pain?

Over time, God mercifully responded to all of my questions as healing and hope were released into my life. It was in this process of healing, however, that two things occurred: (1) God revealed to me His Kingdom principles about suffering; and (2) I was forced to rephrase my questions as I began to understand the relationship between grace and suffering.

## REBELLIOUS SUFFERING

Suffering! Just saying the word can produce a spiritual shudder in our souls because we know that suffering means pain. No one in his right mind wakes up in the morning and thinks—"Please, Lord, make this day as painful as possible."

When I go to the dentist, I don't say, "No, thank you," to the Novocain injection. At that point in my day, I look at the needle as my best friend. I even suggested during a recent root canal that my dentist double the dose.

No, we want to avoid pain and will go to great lengths to protect our physical bodies from harm or injury. At times, we become irrational with safeguards, trying to do anything to protect ourselves and the ones we love. It's as if we're attempting to "tiptoe through the tulips" of life so we can arrive at death safely. How crazy is that? But what does the Bible teach about this important subject? What were the perspectives of Jesus, the apostle Paul and the early church? It's to these questions that we now turn.

I believe the Bible teaches clearly about two types of suffering that we can experience in our walks with God. The first kind is *rebellious suffering*, which I also describe in non-theological language as *stupid suffering*. Rebellious suffering can be defined by the following illustration.

Suppose I'm walking along in my spiritual journey and come to a closed door that intrigues me. I stare at the door and begin to speculate about what might be on the other side. In my fascination, I reach toward the handle so I can open the door and go in. As my hand touches the knob, I hear the inward convicting voice of the Holy Spirit say, "Don't go there, My son." I pull my hand back in obedience, realizing that Jesus doesn't want me to go into that particular room.

"Thank You, Lord, for speaking to me," I say as I continue along my way.

The next day, however, I begin to think about how attractive the door looked. It had been beautifully carved with special inlays, and the handle was especially gorgeous. I start to wonder what incredible things must be waiting on the other side.

In disobedience, I move toward the door again as the conviction of the Spirit comes to my conscience a second time: "Son, don't go there!"

In my frustration, I cry out, "But why, Lord?!"

God is never under obligation to reveal consequences, but maybe in this situation He chooses to share the danger with me: "My son, on the other side of the door, there is a large steel trap that will crush your foot."

"Oh, thank You, Jesus," I respond, backing away from the door in gratitude as I realize that God is watching out for my safety and welfare. I begin to rest in the truth that my genuine freedom is always found within the limitations of what God has created me to be and become. I begin to rest as I walk again in His revealed path.

But the next day, I begin to obsess about the beautiful door as I surrender to the absurd reasoning that I can somehow avoid the trap waiting to crush my foot. *If I open the door quickly enough, I should be able to jump over it,* I scheme in the beginning of my deception. I even start to entertain the insane

> *". . . my genuine freedom is always found within the limitations of what God has created me to be and become."*

thought that God has made this door off-limits because He desires to withhold the very best things from me. Sound familiar?

As I move toward the door a third time, I expect to hear the voice of thunder or experience a spiritual earthquake that will knock me to the ground, and yet I still risk opening it. But nothing happens to deter me as I walk with a sense of triumph to touch the handle and open the door.

My victory is short-lived, for when the beautiful door opens, I am confronted with the largest trap I have ever seen. It immediately springs shut and crushes my right foot with the power of its jagged jaws.

The application of this parable to life is not something that I read in a book. I move today with several spiritual limps that are related to doors I have rebelliously walked through, and the suffering produced by these wayward transgressions is *painfully* real. The healing aftermath and reconstruction of my own "foot" have been devastating to experience, but the spiritual damage was produced by my persistent rebellion. I know I'm not the only one to evidence such stupidity and experience this type of deception.

When we don't heed the Lord's warnings, we can't look at Him and say, "How could You allow this to happen?" or, "Why didn't You warn me?" *When we reject the principles of God's Word, we will always encounter pain and suffering.* This kind of pain is the outworking of rebellion against the Most High God, and it is thrust into our lives as the consequence of violating scriptural principles. God, of course, never abandons us and will always bring healing and restoration as we turn our hearts back to Him. Our affliction in these kinds of circumstances, however, is rooted in spiritual treason, resulting in rebellious suffering.

## REDEMPTIVE SUFFERING

There is a second kind of suffering that we can experience which begins to touch the real essence of life in God's Kingdom. This type can be described as *redemptive suffering.*

It's clear that pain and suffering were a part of the normal Christian life for New Testament believers. Jesus spoke openly about the opposition that we would face as disciples in this world—"'I have chosen you out of the world. That is why the world hates you. Remember the words I spoke to you: "No servant is greater than his master." If they persecuted Me, they will persecute you also'" (John 15:19-20). *The basic essence of true discipleship is following the Lord, and Jesus told all disciples that walking in His footsteps would lead us into paths of unjust suffering.*

The beloved apostle, writing as an exiled prisoner, greeted the churches in Asia Minor with these words: "I, John, your brother and companion in the suffering and Kingdom and patient endurance that are ours in Jesus" (Revelation 1:9). From John's perspective, the experience of suffering (translated in other New Testament passages as tribulation, affliction, distress or anguish) is a part of what it means to be a Christian disciple "in Jesus." He made it crystal clear in verse 9 that his present suffering was "because of the Word of God and the testimony of Jesus."

Christian tradition informs us that, later in his life, John survived the horrific experience of being boiled in oil. It's important to note that these sufferings *were not* the result of walking in disobedience through some restricted doorway. Instead, John was describing pain that entered his life as the direct result of doing the *right* thing. We are talking about a surrendered disciple who was following Jesus with wholehearted devotion as he pursued the will of God for his life.

John was not angry or bitter as he described this suffering in his experience; he simply viewed suffering as a central part of what it meant to be a Christian in God's Kingdom. The reality of suffering will always be found "in Jesus," making it a part of our spiritual DNA.

The apostle Paul provides another powerful example of redemptive suffering. If we are looking for an epitome of what it means to be totally given over to the will of God, we find it in the life of Paul. At times, he seems so completely consumed by Christ's desires that any manifestations of selfishness disappear entirely.

In the second epistle of Corinthians, Paul outlines some of the life experiences he had while walking with Christ in a lifestyle of obedient surrender (11:22-23). Paul begins by describing the hard work that is involved in serving Christ without compromise. He continues by giving testimony to how many times he was beaten for his faith. This happened so often that he lost count, a fact he summarizes with the phrase "times without number."

Paul was beaten with whips and rods and bludgeoned with rocks.

His life was "often in danger." The ship that he was traveling on sank, forcing him to spend over 24 hours with the sharks in open water. So much for traveling mercies!

His journal continues by disclosing the many nights that he was unable to sleep because of hunger and thirst, ". . . often without food in cold and exposure." His testimony becomes especially puzzling when contrasted with the contemporary Christian cliché that "the safest place to be is in the center of God's will," implying we will never be in danger physically or otherwise.

We must maintain a clear perspective as we read Paul's testimony in 2 Corinthians 11. These were real sufferings, involving pain and distress at the highest level. We're talking about actual bloodshed and genuine loss in Paul's life, which is placed against the backdrop of a servant who *is doing* the will of God without compromise.

As we consider together the words of Jesus, John and Paul, we are provided with a description of the differences between the two types of Kingdom suffering. *Rebellious suffering* is the pain I experience as a direct result of resisting and disobeying God. *Redemptive suffering* is the pain I experience as a direct result of loving and obeying God. The contrast is clear, but what makes the second type redemptive? The apostle Peter gives us the answer in his first epistle as he contrasts these two types of suffering (2:18-25).

He begins with the bizarre suggestion that servants should submit not only to masters who are "good and considerate," but "also to those who are harsh" (18). On the surface, this seems to be insane counsel. I am more than willing to submit to a boss who is kind, generous, encouraging and affirming. But submitting to a person who is harsh and unreasonable? Forget it, Peter, I'll pursue a process of litigation instead.

But the apostle persists in his challenge with the following explanation: "For it is commendable if a man bears up under the pain of unjust suffering because he is conscious of God. But how is it to your credit if you receive a beating for doing wrong and endure it? But if you suffer for doing good and you endure it, this is commendable before God" (1 Peter 2:19-20).

It sounds as if Peter is suggesting some kind of Christian masochism where I experience pleasure from the physical and psychological pain inflicted by others. And if I can endure my misery with patience, I have somehow pleased God.

This counsel seems especially repugnant to the current Christian mindset that defines the ultimate goal of existence as choosing a path that gives the greatest amount of personal pleasure and the least amount of pain. The key to understanding this difficult biblical principle is found in the reality of what this kind of suffering *produces* in our lives.

Peter's exhortation culminates with these words in verse 21: "To this you were called, because Christ suffered for you, leaving you an example, that you should follow in His steps." To walk in the path of unjust suffering is literally to walk in the footsteps of Jesus, whose entire life was marked by pristine holiness and purity. He never committed any sin and "no deceit was found in his mouth," and yet He experienced the most intense suffering ever experienced by a human being. The prophetic descriptions of Christ in the book of Isaiah tell us that He would be a "man of sorrows, and acquainted with grief," even adding the startling declaration that the "Lord was pleased to crush Him, putting Him to grief" (53:3, 10).

*"To walk in the path of unjust suffering is literally to walk in the footsteps of Jesus, whose entire life was marked by pristine holiness and purity."*

Here's what I've come to understand: *The amazing redemption that occurs in the experience of unjust suffering is that the character of Christ is formed in my life as I walk in His steps.* It's possible to be changed into His image through the sharing of pain that is undeserved. The heart response that triggers this powerful change in our lives is what the Bible refers to as trust and can be understood only by grappling with the relationship between grace and suffering.

## GRACE AND SUFFERING

The reality of redemptive suffering is offensive to us because it does-n't seem fair. We demand fairness in all of our relationships and activities. Whether we are watching sports, discussing job require-ments or arguing a grade with a teacher, our expectation is that all decisions will be rendered with perfect fairness. In reality, we want *others* to get *exactly* what they deserve.

Fairness generally translates into what will make me feel com-pletely happy and leave me pain-free. I expect to receive from God, my wife, friends and co-workers a treatment that will produce a pam-pered and lovingly nurtured "bubble" around my life.

I especially require this protective bubble in my relationship with God. If I am walking in patterns of obedience, I feel justified in demanding fair compensating treatment because God "owes me" for being such a good son.

If something is wrong with my physical body, it's only fair that Jesus heal me. If I pray in faith about any problem, it's only right that God remove the crisis immediately. After all, if I'm not healed or my financial problems persist, or if my daughter and granddaughter are traumatically uprooted from my life, it's not fair! *I don't deserve this!* my wounded soul screams as redemptive suffering crashes into my world like an unexpected spiritual tsunami.

Several years after the death of our girls, a number of my beloved colleagues experienced the joy of having their first grandchildren. There were effervescent e-mail announcements proclaiming the births of these little ones and friendly ongoing arguments about which baby was more beautiful as digital photographs flew back and forth through cyberspace. I was thrilled with the shared experiences that my friends were having, but in the depth of my heart, nagging questions persisted: Why am I being robbed of these joys? Are my friends more loving, more holy or more committed than I am? Why are these blessings being poured into their lives and not mine? *God, it's just not fair!* I thought.

I believe that this type of "fairness" thinking has become embedded in our North American spiritual consciousness. We have come to see our relationship with God as a working contract where certain blessings are demanded as payment on His part in exchange for faith and upright behavior on ours. It's as though we believe God owes us corresponding and appropriate compensation because it's fair.

These deeply rooted attitudes and expectations demonstrate that we neither appreciate nor understand the grace of God. The first fundamental truth about grace is that God desires to give me a salvation, which I *don't* deserve. The miracle of the Cross is that the punishment and death I *do* deserve have already been poured out on Christ. In a selfless, chosen act of grace, He exchanged His righteous purity for my sinful pollution, and I am completely forgiven.

In 2 Corinthians 5:21, Paul says, "God made Him who had no sin to be sin for us, so that in Him we might become the righteousness of God." We must emphasize Paul's incredible point that we have absorbed and *become* God's righteousness only because Christ has absorbed and *become* our sin. As Jesus hung between heaven and earth, He received into His pure, sinless body all of the rebellion, pollution and darkness for which we should be punished.

> *"The astoundingly strange answer is that the most evil person was the Holy One who never committed a sinful thought or act."*

We've all heard people question who was the most evil person to live on Planet Earth. Was it Jezebel, Bloody Mary, Hitler, Stalin, Milosevic or Hussein? The astoundingly strange answer is that the most evil person was the Holy One who never committed a sinful thought or act.

You see, salvation is more than the transfer of God's righteousness to me; it's also the transfer of my sinful impurity to Christ, which accomplishes the marvelous exchange of grace. So, when I stand before the Holy God of the universe, the last thing I want is fairness because that would demand my condemnation, punishment and death. Instead, when Christ and His sacrifice are embraced in faith, I am able to stand as a trophy of grace, having received a forgiveness that I didn't deserve.

There is no way that this understanding of grace can be disconnected from the whole fabric of my life experience. I am able to enjoy a relationship with Christ today only because God made a decision to treat me unfairly. The Cross, of course, does not negate God's perfect justice because Christ has been judged in my place (Romans 3:25-27). This incredible love causes me daily to receive the extravagant grace of God as He pours forth His blessings into my undeserving life.

The cry that comes from our hearts during the experience of redemptive suffering is, "It's not fair," or, "I don't deserve this." Sometimes, we take it a step further in our process of self-examination and demand an answer—*Why me, Lord?* This type of thinking is basically demanding that God create a spiritual dichotomy in our lives. Without realizing, we're exacting, "Give me what I don't deserve when it will make me comfortable and happy, but only what I do deserve when it comes to suffering and pain."

The truth, of course, is that we can't have it both ways because God's grace is extended to all the parts of our lives. We live in a fallen world, having been flawed by the sinful rebellion described in Genesis 3. Our destinies must be fulfilled in an abnormal world that is not the way God created it to be. This fact alone means all of our lives will be invaded at times by events that are unfair. Sometimes, bad things really do happen to good people.

I've learned that, when unjust suffering makes its traumatic, shattering intrusion into my life (as it did with Jesus, John and Paul), I must rephrase the questions that pour out of my soul. Instead of entreating, "Why *me*, Lord?" I can risk trusting in the mystery of His grace by saying, "Why *not* me, Lord?"

Job, in the midst of his awful pain, expressed an understanding of this relationship between grace and suffering with the following words: "'Shall we accept good from God, and not trouble?'" (Job 2:10). The tension that exists between these two realities of undeserved blessing and undeserved suffering finds its resolution by surrendering in trust the *why* questions to God.

## FAITH AND TRUST

We previously stated that trust is the catalyst which triggers character change as I experience redemptive suffering in my life. When I am decimated with pain that I don't deserve and continue to follow Christ, I am truly walking in His steps as I am transformed into His image. Peter goes so far as to say, "To this you were called, because Christ suffered for you, leaving you an example, that you should follow in His steps" (1 Peter 2:21).

How did our Lord respond when He experienced this kind of unjust suffering? Peter gives us the simple yet profound answer with these words: ". . . when He suffered, He made no threats. Instead, He entrusted Himself to Him who judges justly" (23).

This attitude of Christ models a powerful truth principle: Either we lash out at Jesus and others as we blame them for the hurt that has blown up our lives, or we entrust our lives to God in the midst of pain that we do not understand. Such a heart response of trust produces redemptive change and healing. We'll have more to say about this in future chapters. For the moment, we'll examine the subtle but important differences that exist between faith and trust.

Without question, Hebrews 11 is *the* faith chapter of the Bible. The list of biblical heroes that is paraded before us is a "who's who" catalogue of women and men who "conquered kingdoms" and "put foreign armies to flight" (33-34).

Each of the stories of these faith champions is marked by significant diversity. The story of Abraham is different from the testimony of Moses. Sarah's life experience is a radical contrast to the account of Rahab's salvation and deliverance. In spite of these greatly diverse experiences, however, we can still discover two common denominators shared by each of our heroes.

First, we can say that true faith can never be expressed without taking dramatic risk. Without exception, the risk of faith is illustrat-

*". . . we can say that true faith can never be expressed without taking dramatic risk."*

ed powerfully in all of the exemplary lives recorded for us in Hebrews 11. The challenge of faith risk is clearly defined by the following question that confronts all believers in their walks

with God: Are we willing to lay down our lives for a reality that we do not see (11:1)?

Rahab provides us with a terrific illustration. She was willing to stand against her entire culture by protecting the spies as she awaited deliverance behind a scarlet cord, believing in faith for a military victory that was yet to be won. To the natural eye, Rahab would be seen as unrealistic and unstable.

"Let's get practical," we would shout at her in the twenty-first century. "How can anyone risk his or her life for something unseen which cannot be proved scientifically in advance?" Our analytical minds demand a sure guarantee, or we are unable to move forward with confidence and assurance.

This type of faith risk raises an important question: Why would anyone risk the future and her very way of life for something not yet seen? The answer brings us to the second area of common ground that links together the varied experiences of our Hebrews 11 heroes. *Each one of them took the risking leap of faith in obedient response to a clear word from God.* This is why true faith pleases God, because He sees our commitment and abandonment to the word He has spoken. Without this risk, it "is impossible to please Him" (11:6).

The life of Rahab again provides us with an example. Why was she willing to risk her life as she disconnected from her culture and her people? What motivated her radical decisions and actions as she waited for the fulfillment of an unseen promise?

Rahab was committed to take any risk because God had spoken His word to her heart. In her interaction with the two spies, she made the following declaration: "'. . . the Lord your God is God in heaven above and on earth below'" (Joshua 2:11). Where did this understanding about Joshua's God come from? How was it possible for a prostitute in a wicked city to arrive at such a solid biblical truth when it had taken the covenant people almost 40 years to come to the same conclusion?

It appears Rahab's astounding declaration arose from some insight or word of the Lord that had come privately and personally to her heart. She must have had some heart revelation of who God was for her to have made such an assertion. God must have been speaking to this woman that He loved, and in an act of responsive faith, she risked everything because she believed His word was true. There was no scientific guarantee, but she moved in "the assurance of things hoped for," with "the conviction of things not seen" (Hebrews 11:1, NASB).

We can see from Hebrews 11 that the two common connecting themes of faith are related to radical risk-taking in response to the word that God has spoken. But how are we to understand the experience of trust?

The response of trust (to which we made passing reference in chapter one) is best illustrated in the testimony of three young men in the book of Daniel. Hananiah, Mishael and Azariah were caught up in an intense political and spiritual crisis as they faced a choice that might have cost them their lives. Would they bow to the image of Nebuchadnezzar, or would they be thrown into a blazing furnace that had been heated seven times hotter than normal (Daniel 3:19)? I might add that the heat of this fire was so severe that the men escorting the Hebrews to their attempted execution were themselves killed by its intensity.

The choice these men faced was very straightforward: Bow to the image or die! Nebuchadnezzar was quick to point out that there was no god who could deliver them out of his hands (Daniel 3:15).

The response of Hananiah and his friends was classic when they confronted the king with these words: "'. . . the God we serve is able to save us from it, and He will rescue us from your hand, O king. But even if He does not . . . we will not serve your gods . . .'" (17-18).

May I suggest that Hananiah, Mishael and Azariah *did not* respond with faith in this situation? They didn't because faith is always responding to a word that God has *previously* spoken. If God had promised to deliver them, then their faith would have proclaimed, "Throw us in because we will come out alive." They didn't say that. Remember, they said, "'But even if He does not . . . .'"

God had not given them any such word. They knew that God *was able* to deliver, they just weren't completely sure that He *would* deliver them. This evidences they trusted God, and their heart attitude was that of the surrender of trust.

As we bring together these two realities of faith and trust, I believe we can make the following distinctions. *Faith means risking obedience after God has spoken.* I am willing to die for the promise that He has given to me.

> "Without faith, it is impossible to truly please God. Without trust, it is impossible to truly love Him."

*Trust, on the other hand, means risking surrender before God has spoken.* I am willing to die because God has proven His love and faithfulness in the past.

Without faith, it is impossible to truly please God. Without trust, it is impossible to truly love Him.

Let's summarize the themes of this chapter as we apply them to the pain and loss we experience in our lives.

## SUMMARY

**Suffering is a part of the *normal* Christian life**. It can occur because I have rebelled against God in defiant disobedience, or it can come while I am walking in a loving, committed relationship with King Jesus.

**Suffering is not an abnormality.** Properly understood, suffering becomes part of the basic definition of *true spirituality*.

Unjust suffering occurs because I live in a fallen, flawed world, and it can become powerfully redemptive as it produces the character of Christ in me. When I experience unjust suffering, I am only following in the steps of Christ, the apostles and countless disciples through the centuries who have paved the way.

That being said, we must never feel God is emotionally detached from our lives as we encounter the reality of pain and loss. He is intimately involved in *all* that we experience. As the writer of Hebrews tells us, "We do not have a high priest who is unable to sympathize with our weaknesses, but we have one who has been tempted in every way, just as we are—yet was without sin." On that basis, we can "approach the throne of grace with confidence, so that we may receive mercy and find grace to help us in our time of need" (Hebrews 4:15-16).

Salvation has provided a love relationship with a Savior who carries us on His shoulders *and* close to His heart, having experienced in His own body the same unjust afflictions we are encountering. David understood and beautifully expressed this truth when he said: "Thou hast taken account of my wandering; put my tears in thy bottle; are they not in Thy book?" (Psalm 56:8, NASB).

I have been deeply moved by that verse when I have reflected on the river of tears personally shed over the loss of my daughter and granddaughter. I have the comforting image of Father God gathering up each precious tear, placing them in His bottle and recording them in His "book of tears." God is not seated in the heavens wearing a starched white lab coat as He clinically observes our pain like some scientific experiment. He hurts with us and intimately feels our every sob.

**Grace and suffering are closely intertwined in the package of salvation that Christ has provided for us.** Our redemption and forgiveness are made possible only through the "riches of His grace that He lavished on us" (Ephesians 1:7-8).

The foundation for every blessing I have ever received is built on grace and grace *alone*. Continually, God has given me in kindness what I don't deserve. When unjust suffering blindsides me and knocks me to the ground, I must reach out in trust to embrace the same empowering grace.

God has proven His faithfulness to me over and over again; so in blessing and pain, I must trust grace to work out His eternal plan and purpose for my life.

**We must surrender the *why* questions to God in trust if we ever hope to find comfort, healing and growth**. *Faith* is able to embrace final answers because God has spoken clearly. *Trust* is able to embrace God in the absence of any answers at all.

I began this chapter by sharing certain *why* questions that flooded into my heart. Why would God allow this horrible tragedy? Why didn't God respond to the prayers of so many committed Christian believers? Why didn't God empower the physicians to work a medical miracle? These types of questions and their corresponding footnotes could be asked continuously for the rest of my life.

At the funeral, my friend and mentor, Paul Johansson, gave a short reflection just before our daughter's pastor shared the message. As he looked compassionately at our family, he said: "This is a most difficult day, and the *only* one *not* asking why is René."

That profoundly simple statement put everything in perspective. René was in the presence of Jesus, the One she had loved and served. She had entered into the joy of her eternal inheritance, and there were no *why* questions burning on her lips. For the ones who loved her so deeply, however, the *whys* were exploding like shrapnel in our souls.

The final surrender of trust is making peace with the reality that certain questions will *never* be answered on this side of eternity. Answers *do* exist, but God in His wisdom will sometimes withhold information at key crossroads in our lives. These divine silences require a personal response on our part. We can demand answers or even walk away from God in bitterness of soul and find another god to serve. Or, in the grip of debilitating pain with unanswered *why* questions still churning in our hearts, we can choose to trust and, over time, receive His peace, comfort and healing.

In the midst of devastating losses, we are called to walk in the "valley of the shadow of death." I believe this difficult walk involves a *process* that brings us to a second principle and the focus of our next chapter.

# CHAPTER 3

# God's Process

### *Principle 2:*
### *Comfort, healing, restoration and a beautiful end are all fruit of our embracing God and the grief process.*

O ne characteristic of North American culture is we demand results immediately. If we are caught in traffic, we become irritated and frustrated, perhaps to the point of acting out in road rage. Other motorists seem willing to ram us while attempting to force themselves between our grill and the bumper of the next automobile. I have personally witnessed tragic accidents on interstate highways because motorists have not been content to travel within the flow of 75 miles an hour in a passing lane.

Yes, we're an impatient people, desiring instant gratification. Even when our computers don't take us to the desired Web site in ten seconds or less, we are ready to upgrade for faster models. I confess I recently stood before my own microwave oven, restless with impatience, because it was taking more than two minutes to reheat my rice and beans.

It's unfortunate when these demanding expectations for speed are transferred over into our love relationship with Christ. In our walks with God, we find ourselves demanding immediate results. We pray at 7:00 and expect a clear answer and change by 7:05. If God created the entire world in six days, then He should surely solve our problems in five minutes or less, right?

## PEACE, PRAYER AND TIME

Paul gives us the following exhortation in his letter to the Philippian church: "Do not be anxious about anything, but in everything, by prayer and petition, with thanksgiving, present your requests to God" (Philippians 4:6). This statement captures a basic life principle for believers: *We are commanded to pray and petition the Lord about everything that touches our lives.*

Paul, however, continues in this passage by giving a wonderful promise. If we pray about everything, then God's peace, "which transcends all understanding," will guard our hearts and minds "in Christ Jesus" (7).

The relationship between peace and prayer must always be connected to the process of time. If God answered all prayers immediately and gave us what we wanted, then there would be no need for imparted peace to stand guard over our hearts and minds. If we prayed yesterday and got our desired answer today, then there would be no need for supernatural peace. We'd simply receive the answer and move on with our lives, rejoicing that God was able to see things our way. If, however, God tells us no or gives us an unexpected answer, or perhaps no answer at all, then we suddenly find ourselves in desperate need of God's imparted peace.

*"God is able to accomplish immediate change in our lives if He desires, but He is also committed to the process of change."*

My personal spiritual heritage is rich in testimonies of what God is able to do instantly in a person's life at a church altar. I have participated in thousands of meetings in over 30 years of active ministry, many of them concluding with invitations for believers to come forward to receive prayer. I believe unequivocally that God is able to bring dramatic and *immediate* change through prayer. No prophet said it more clearly than Jeremiah when he declared: "'Ah, Sovereign Lord, You have made the heavens and the earth by Your great power and outstretched arm. Nothing is too hard for You'" (Jeremiah 32:17). God is able to accomplish immediate change in our lives if He desires, but He is also committed to the process of change.

## CHANGE'S GRADUAL PROCESS

The process of change is demonstrated in the patterns of normal spiritual growth. We are "being transformed into His likeness with ever-increasing glory" as we walk with Him in daily relationship (2 Corinthians 3:18).

The metaphor of the fruit of the Spirit also teaches us about the process of change. Fruit does not grow overnight but undergoes a cycle of transformation that produces maturity and harvest. Although I believed otherwise when I was in my twenties, I have modified my "speed theology" with the conviction that God is *never* in a hurry.

One illustration of this principle is seen in God's covenant with Abraham when He explains that there will be a divine delay in the final fulfillment of the promise because the "'sin of the Amorites has not yet reached its full measure'" (Genesis 15:16). What kind of delay is God talking about?

An Old Testament chronology from the Abrahamic covenant to the conquest of Canaan would put the gap at about 675 years. God could have compressed these years if He had so desired because He is the Creator of time and stands as Lord over it. But His purposes were served more perfectly by allowing almost 700 years to transpire while extending extravagant grace to multiple generations. I also believe that the reality of *gradual process* has direct application to physical and emotional healing. By way of illustration, I'll share a story from my childhood.

When I was nine years old, I was following two of my female class-mates home from school. I was totally in love with one of the little girls and was convinced that she would grow up to be my wife. The object of my affection acted as though I didn't exist, providing a source of great distress in my private world at that time. That particular afternoon intensified my misery because an older bully was picking on both of the girls by continually throwing an empty Coca-Cola bottle at them. They were both pleading with him to stop, but he responded by throwing the bottle even harder. I clearly saw the opportunity to be a great hero and win the affection of my imagined little girlfriend.

In a moment of daring courage, I inserted my body between the girls and the giant who was four years older than I. "Stop throwing that bottle," I demanded, looking up several stories into his angry face.

"Who's gonna stop me?" he shouted back, as he raised the bottle like a club to strike me.

I realized immediately I hadn't developed a strategic leadership plan, but in a flash of brilliant inspiration, I snatched the bottle from his hand and threw it against an adjacent brick wall. The bottle exploded like a glass grenade into my left kneecap, cutting my leg to the bone as I collapsed to the sidewalk in a pool of my own blood.

In the midst of my pain, I experienced a brief moment of triumph as I watched the bully run away in horror. My victory was short-lived, however, as I watched the girl of my dreams heartlessly abandon me in my hour of need.

The hours and days that followed my accident remain vivid in my mind. I remember the pain that I felt at the hospital as the doctor meticulously cleaned the glass fragments from my open wound. My mother went into a dead faint as they began to stitch me up. I can remember lying in my bed at home that evening, fighting back the tears for hours because of the anguish I felt from the injury. I would have found it hard to believe on that Friday evening my pain had only just begun.

A week later, I woke in the morning to find that my knee had swollen to twice its normal size because the wound had become infected. At the doctor's office, our family physician proceeded to

lance my knee so that the infection could be drained and real healing could begin. The pain I felt during that excruciating surgical
procedure made the first evening at the hospital seem minor. The
principle emerging here has clear application to any area of emotional healing: *If a wound becomes infected, it cannot heal properly and will
cause greater pain and harm than the original injury.*

The healing of my childhood injury occurred over a process of
time. Over 50 years later, I can remember the accident because of a
visible scar on my left knee. I know, however, that I received a gradual physical healing. How do I know? By two present realities in my
life today: I can walk, *and* the wound doesn't hurt anymore.

There is a profound spiritual correlation of these principles to
the process of emotional healing that occurs in our lives. We experience (sometimes suddenly) a horrendous wound that literally
knocks us to the ground. In the midst of debilitating pain, we wonder if we'll ever be able to spiritually walk again.

Sometimes, emotional wounds become infected, and more hurt
is experienced on the pathway to wholeness. The loss of our daughter and granddaughter produced a deep wound that left a scar on
all the members of our family. We'll always be aware of the scar, *but*
the Holy Spirit has brought true healing into all of our lives. Our
anguish has been dramatically reduced, and there are many days
that pass where we're not even aware of any pain at all. More impor-
tantly, we're able to walk in normal patterns of spiritual growth with
the Lord whom we love and serve, but this present healing was
imparted as a *gradual process.*

The deafening cacophony of our pain made it difficult to hear
the voice of the Lord in the aftermath of the funeral. Christ's spoken
beatitude in Matthew 5:4 was one of the few Scriptures that broke
through the thick fog of our grief: "'Blessed are those who mourn,
for they will be comforted.'" The application of these words to our family became crystal clear. *Jesus was promising comfort and healing as fruit
of the mourning process.* The true supernatural healing and comfort of

His Spirit would be available to us only as we embraced this process of mourning. Without mourning, there would be no true comfort.

In walking the path of grief during the last decade, I have come to understand two truths that describe how we experience this gradual reality of healing. First, we must embrace the process of grief and mourning. And second, we must apply the principles of biblical covenant to human suffering.

Let's consider more closely these principles in light of the losses we experience as we walk with God.

## EMBRACING THE PROCESS OF GRIEF AND MOURNING

True healing always starts with absolute honesty. Any parroted clichés that attempt to minimize the agony we feel in devastating loss are empty and offensive. We experience true comfort only as we embrace, without compromise, the mourning process.

The process begins with the *honest* recognition of the pain that invades our whole being in the experience of suffering. Most hospital rooms are equipped with a pain graph on the wall, assisting doctors, nurses and patients to identify the intensity of the pain that occurs after surgery. The nurse will stand at the foot of the bed and ask the patient to describe his pain on a scale of one through ten. The response that is given enables the medical team to assess the person's ongoing recovery and to make necessary adjustments in the administration of pain medication. If a patient is not honest about his pain, he can sabotage his own recovery.

This principle also applies to the emotional pain we experience in life. If we deny the presence of pain, we cut ourselves off from the reality of God's comfort.

After the death of my girls, the intensity of my anguish seemed to be "off the pain chart." The number *ten* seemed hardly adequate to measure the excruciating and debilitating pain I lived with every day. I came to identify strongly with the cry of Job—"'If only my anguish could be weighed and all my misery be placed on the scales! It would surely outweigh the sand of the seas . . .'" (Job 6:2-3).

My honest and *gradual* healing had to begin by facing the biblical truth that "hope deferred makes the heart sick" (Proverbs 13:12). I realized incrementally how seriously ill my heart had become in the struggle with "deferred hope." As I wrestled with the losses that occurred on my Black Friday, it seemed as though God's hand had reached intrusively into my life and erased a great part of my future.

*"If we deny the presence of pain, we cut ourselves off from the reality of God's comfort."*

I had stored certain treasures of hope in my heart that I believed were a part of God's future blessing for my life. One scenario I had played over and over again in my mind was René's bringing my granddaughter to me while I sat in a rocking chair, happily anticipating her placing little Jessica into my arms for the first time. I had seen myself rocking her gently as I dedicated her to the Lord with tears of joy. I had believed with all of my heart that I *would* have that wonderful experience. But in the space of one hour on a snowy March night, this part of my future disappeared with a finality that rocked the very foundations of my life.

My loved ones were gone, and they were never coming back. I knew the Scriptures, and I understood theologically that my girls had not been *taken* but *received* into the very presence of Jesus. I also knew beyond any shadow of doubt that I would be reunited with them in heaven. But I recognized with equal certainty that particular precious hopes had been dashed and deferred for *life*, leaving me with a sick heart that made it difficult to breathe.

I had begun to encounter profound emotions born of grief, learning by experience an important lesson about confessing pain: *When we honestly acknowledge the reality of our pain, we become free to grapple with five powerful emotions.* These emotions must be confronted directly because they pull on our hearts like powerful Atlantic rip currents.

## Shock

The first emotion that demands confrontation is the *shock* of grief. Shock manifests itself with feelings of being dazed and stunned, especially during the immediate aftermath of loss. I believe that shock is God's way of protecting us from the overwhelming reality of pain exploding in our lives.

Let me reflect on the experience of shock in connection with the childhood injury to my knee. While I was being transported to the hospital, my mother kept changing bath towels that were soaked with my blood. Staring down in detachment at the deep wound on my leg, I remember thinking, *This should really hurt.* I didn't realize then that shock was insulating me from a pain that would have overwhelmed me.

At my daughter's funeral, I had a similar spiritual experience. As our son-in-law closed the casket, triggering the beginning of the service, I felt the Holy Spirit envelope me with pillows of surreal comfort. In the natural, I should have been screaming, but shock came as a gift of grace, making it possible for me to move forward.

## Confusion

The second powerful emotion that swirled within my broken heart was the *confusion* of grief. In the aftereffects of loss, confusion forcefully inserts itself into our shattered world. This confusion becomes greatly magnified as we try to reconcile our personal loss with the sure promises of God.

In the next chapter, we'll discuss in more detail the paradox and tension between faith and unanswered prayer. Here, it's mentioned in connection with the early stages of grief. In these stages, we wonder how we can believe in a loving God who is committed to blessing us when we feel smashed by an excruciating pain that He *could* have prevented.

The confusion surrounding such bewilderment becomes especially disorienting as we experience difficulty in completing the necessary tasks and functions of our everyday lives. I found myself, for example, struggling with a debilitating lethargy that expressed itself with the attitude of indifference. I thought, *What difference does it make whether I do this or not?* This confusion robs us of our spiritual and emotional equilibrium as we vicariously echo Job's protest—"'The arrows of the Almighty are in me, my spirit drinks in their poison . . .'" (6:4).

### Anxiety

Another common emotion in the early stages of loss is the *anxiety* of grief. This anxiety is irrational and crippling to faith.

After the death of my girls, I continued to move in the spiritual leadership of my position, and I remember clearly the moment in an evening service when I was asked to pray for a person needing physical healing. As I began to petition the Lord, I felt overcome with a deep anxiety that swallowed up my faith. I prayed all of the right words, but I didn't really believe anything would happen. I recall thinking that, if God made a choice not to heal my daughter, why would it be any different in this particular situation?

This anxiety opened the door to the fear that other people I loved would die also. Six weeks after the death of my daughter, I was driving to the yearly Junior/Senior Banquet for our Bible college. Our younger daughter, a member of the senior class, was already enroute to the banquet center with a group of her classmates. As my wife and I crested a hill on the road our students were traveling, we saw ambulances, police cars and fire trucks responding to a horrific motor vehicle accident. All traffic was being rerouted because the state police had closed the highway. I got out of the car and approached one of the officers. "I'm the Dean of students at Elim," I explained, "and it's very possible that some of our students might be involved in this accident. Could you please let me drive up and check?"

He agreed and radioed ahead to the other members of the rescue team. I jumped in my car and began to proceed towards the accident with a prayer on my lips. My prayer stuck in my throat, however, as I suddenly remembered my daughter was traveling on this very road. *That would be impossible,* I thought. *God would never allow another tragic death in our family.* It gives me deep pain to share the thought that came next. *Of course, He would,* I almost said aloud. *That would be just like Him.*

As I approached the accident scene, I fully expected to see the body of my younger daughter lying on the ground. In fact, the crash did not involve any of our students, although it did claim the precious life of a lady in our village community.

As I drove away from the site, I found myself crying out to the Lord for His forgiveness. "How can I think this way about You?" I said through my tears. "I know You are a good God. Please help me to move again in a confident, faith-filled relationship with You."

Although God answered that prayer in the months ahead, there were still many battles to be fought in this war between faith and the anxiety of grief.

### Anger

A fourth emotion that dramatically inserts itself through the losses of life is the *anger* of grief. For a committed Christian, this can be the most difficult emotion to admit because we have been conditioned to see all anger as sinful and unhealthy.

I have been engaged in pastoral counseling situations where I have made the observation, "You seem to be very angry about this."

Immediately, the agitated response is fired back in my face, "Oh, I'm not angry!"

The face is flushed, the body is rigid, and the blood pressure elevated, but "No, we're not angry!" Genuine healing can never occur without the honest acknowledgment of this powerful emotion.

The multiple and diverse losses we experience in life are accompanied by a desire to protest. *This can't be happening to me! This shouldn't have happened to me! God, how could You have allowed this to happen?* These are our attempts at protest.

After my daughter's funeral, I had to get honest about the anger in my own heart. I remember one time of prayer when I said, "Lord, I am angry at You for allowing this." I may not have shaken my fist at the heavens, but that gesture would certainly have captured the attitude of my heart.

I discovered in amazement, though, that God was big enough to handle my anger, and it came as no surprise to Him, anyway, because He intimately knows me. When anger is nurtured and allowed to take root, however, it becomes destructive and produces bitterness in our lives. Instead, if anger is openly acknowledged and surrendered to the person of the Holy Spirit, it becomes redemptive in helping us to embrace the reality of our loss.

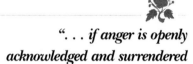

*". . . if anger is openly acknowledged and surrendered to the person of the Holy Spirit, it becomes redemptive in helping us to embrace the reality of our loss."*

## Sadness

Another emotional wave that seeks to overwhelm us in loss is the *sadness* of grief. When we lose someone or something, we hurt. We even may not realize just how deeply we hurt at the onset of our loss. My family did not fully encounter the depths of our sadness for several months. This slow progression was vital because, if we had felt everything at once, our pain would have overwhelmed us.

It's important for us to understand that our bodies are affected by sadness. In fact, physiological changes commonly occur when we experience sadness. The body actually responds over time to the impact of loss. The most common physical reactions are insomnia and exhaustion. Muscle pain, shortness of breath, emptiness in the stomach, nausea, headaches, weight loss or gain, agitation, anxiety and tension are just some of the other ways our bodies may respond to the experience of catastrophic pain. *It's only over time that body, soul and spirit are able to work together in a way that allows us to embrace the full intensity of our pain.*

## UNPREDICTABILITY

In addition to these five emotions, there are also certain principles that provide a road map for the healing journey. It's important first we recognize grief is *unpredictable*. Grief is often described in books, journals and other writing as an orderly process that moves according to predictable stages and patterns, but this type of thinking paints an incorrect and misleading picture.

The unpredictable pattern of sorrow is directly connected to the relationship between grief and mourning. Grief is the sum total of all of the feelings, thoughts and pain we feel within ourselves. Grief is *internal*. Mourning, on the other hand, is the *external* expression of what we feel on the inside. Crying, talking about the loss or celebrating special anniversary dates provides a few examples of mourning.

After the death of a loved one, friends sometimes encourage us to keep our grief to ourselves. *Healing can be experienced, however, only when we begin to mourn publicly in the presence of understanding and caring people who will not judge us.*

Talking about orderly stages of grief somehow seems to comfort people as they try to make sense of death and loss. *If only I can get through these first stages,* we may think to ourselves, *I'll be okay.*

The truth is there is no logical progression that makes grief predictable. It's turbulent and comes without warning, bouncing here and there, and sometimes skipping stages altogether. Walking through grief is like getting into the ocean on a day when there is strong surf. There can be momentary lulls that seduce us into turning our backs and relaxing, only to be suddenly knocked off our feet by a new wave that catches us unaware.

## INDIVIDUALITY

A second important principle is expressed with the truth that grief is highly *personal and individual,* taking on its own shape, size and termination point. After the death of our girls, my wife and I had cause to reflect on the 50% divorce rate statistic for couples experiencing the death of a child. In our pastoral counseling, we had actually challenged the accuracy of such statistics on numerous occasions. As we walked through the grief process together, however, we realized that the statistical percentage was probably not an exaggeration.

In all of the other trials and tests that we had encountered in our years of marriage, one of us had always been in a position to encourage the other. In the throes of our grief walk, though, we felt we had nothing to give *or* say to one another. It's difficult to lean on someone who is already doubled over in pain. As we clung together in our grief, our only response was trying to understand what the other person was experiencing.

I, for example, was able to move more easily in the public dimension of our ministry as we journeyed into the second year of the healing process. Connie found the public demands almost unbearable. There was no formula or blueprint to keep us on the same page in our grief walk through the dark "valley of the shadow." We supported one another in our prayer and love, but each experienced a very personal path as we opened our hearts to the comfort of the Holy Spirit.

My sister, Pam, after losing her husband to cancer, would weekly visit his gravesite on a Saturday morning. She'd take fresh flowers and spend time in prayer as she imagined a one-way conversation with her beloved husband, who had crossed over into the arms of Jesus. This personalized mourning continued for two years and was very healing for her.

By way of contrast, to this day, my wife and I have never been emotionally able to visit the grave where our daughter and granddaughter are buried. There is no right or wrong in the healing path of grief and mourning because it's unpredictable and highly personal.

### PROPORTIONALITY

There is a third principle which serves as a milepost marker in the healing process: Our depth of grief will always be in direct proportion to the depth of love that we had for the person who was lost. A person who hasn't loved deeply will never grieve deeply.

This reality is demonstrated by the losses we become acquainted with every day. We pick up the newspaper and read about a teenager who was killed in an auto accident while driving under the influence. For the moment, our hearts are torn as we pray for the family and try to enter their world of pain. But three days later, we have gone on with our lives and forgotten the incident. Why? Because the people were not intimately connected or related to us. The grieving family and friends, however, are only beginning a journey that will mark them for life.

*"Our depth of grief will always be in direct proportion to the depth of love that we had for the person who was lost."*

The depth of our pain is always related to the depth of our love. The intensity of our grief is measured by how vulnerable we were to the other person, how much we gave of ourselves and how much respect and commitment we poured into the relationship. That is why the loss of divorce brings the pain of death into a person's life, because covenant love has been severed.

With the loss of our daughter, I became sensitized in part to the unique grief my wife was experiencing because Connie had carried René for nine months in her body. There was a special bond formed between them at the moment of conception, and it had continued to strengthen until the day of our daughter's death. As her father, I too had my own special bond with her. Consequently, our river of grief flowed in very deep channels because of the love we had shared together and individually in 24 years of relationship with her.

## TIME

It's also critical in the healing process to understand the following biblical principle, which our friend, Sylvia, also shared with us: "Time doesn't heal, but Jesus heals over time."

Throughout our lives, we had heard many variations on the theme of healing time. Here is a sampling of some statements people spoke to us in our grief: "Time is a great healer," or, "Time will make everything better," or, "Things will get better with the passing of time."

All of these phrases are fundamentally flawed because they assign both personality and power to time. There is a sense in which time *can exert* a powerful influence over our lives. We speak of the tyranny of the urgent, for example, and we all feel the demand of full schedules that have to be formatted to accommodate the limitations of 24-hour days. There is nothing more unforgiving than time. Although we recognize the seeds of truth contained in all of these concepts, the fundamental reality remains that time has no power to promote or create emotional healing in anyone's life.

In actuality, the exact opposite can be true. If a person does not respond with right choices in the crisis of personal pain, a root of bitterness can potentially be planted. Bitterness can grow in a person's life for months and years, turning the individual into a hardened, caustic, toxic, untouchable shell. I believe the ministry of the Holy Spirit is the only reality that provides complete healing, restoration and revival for a decimated heart.

*Either healing or bitterness will be produced, not by the power of time, but rather by the choices we make in embracing or resisting the person of the Holy Spirit who comes to us in the grief process.* I believe that the book of Nehemiah provides us with some clear perspectives as to how this process is worked out.

## CHOICES

In Nehemiah, we have an account of the children of Israel return-ing to the devastated land that once was filled with the glory of God. The condition of Jerusalem is now desperate. What was once a strong, beautiful city is now reduced to piles of rubble. Though referring to a city, this is also a descriptive image of a personal life shattered by loss, where order and joy are replaced by chaos and pain.

In the early part of our own grief walk, Connie and I were keen-ly aware that visible wounds and scars had marred the former beau-ty of our lives. As we stood in the rubble that was left behind, our pain was exacerbated by the memories of the way things used to be. Now when we read Nehemiah's story, we can identify with him and his people.

When Nehemiah is made aware of the distress and devastation of the great city of Jerusalem, he is moved with deep emotion, saying, "When I heard these things, I sat down and wept. For some days I mourned and fasted and prayed before the God of heaven" (1:4). With these words, Nehemiah describes the foundation of grief and mourn-ing. For us as well, when our lives are overwhelmed by the reality of painful loss, it's important that we have the freedom to *weep* for days.

But even with the awareness of all this devastation and rubble, Nehemiah does more than weep. He begins to pray that the all-redeeming God will somehow make a way for restoration to occur. His prayer produces an audience with the king where he asks to be sent to the city of his fathers so he can "rebuild" it (2:5).

The Lord answers Nehemiah's prayer and allows him to return to Jerusalem. As he physically stands among the ruins of Jerusalem's walls, he is confronted with the following question: Can the broken pieces be put back together in a way that will reflect new beauty and order? Is it possible that his weeping can be turned into joy?

The *yes* answers to these questions are founded on the concepts of hard work *and* aggressively battling the forces that resist the rebuilding process. *Nehemiah teaches us that severe resistance will always challenge the rebuilding and restorative work in our lives.*

There is a real enemy who wars against our souls, and he does not want to see us healed. Although I believe in a real Devil and demons, I do not look for them around every spiritual corner. As we discussed in the previous chapter, our lives belong to Christ, who decisively defeated Satan through His Cross and resurrection. But the Good Shepherd Himself warns us that "'the thief comes only to steal and kill and destroy'" (John 10:10). Jesus states it so plainly: There is a *real* thief that seeks to hurt and demolish our lives.

I believe that this thieving enemy is especially active in a commitment to *resist* the healing process in broken, hurting people and to keep us imprisoned in the rubble and devastation of our pain. The book of Nehemiah gives us some key perspectives that help us to understand *and* battle this intense resistance.

The first perspective makes us aware of the *anger* of the enemy. Nehemiah's enemy is a man, named Sanballat, who becomes furious and very angry when he hears the Jews are rebuilding the wall. Interestingly, two different Hebrew words are used in connection with the anger of Sanballat. The Hebrew word, *charah*, means to literally "glow with anger." The second word, *kaac*, speaks of a "heated heart" that leads a person to destructive action. This is Satan's attitude as he opposes the rebuilding and restoration process in our lives. His resistance is always rooted in heated, destructive anger.

*"Where there is no hope for the future, there is no power for the present."*

This intense anger is then vented and demonstrated by asking subtle questions intended to bring *discouragement*. Discouragement is one of the most powerful tools of the enemy because it can cause a person to give up. In this connection, the Lord has made the following truth forcefully real to my heart: Where there is no hope for the future, there is no power for the present.

The first question designed to rob hope and bring discouragement is related to the area of strength. Sanballat challenges the people as he asks: "'What are those *feeble* Jews doing?'" (Nehemiah 4:2, emphasis added). By implication, he is suggesting it will be impossible for the people to rebuild because of their physical weakness.

In the aftermath of grief, we are confronted with the same kind of thought patterns. We are acutely aware of the emotional weakness that has been produced in our brokenness, making it so easy to agree with the implanted thoughts of the enemy and just *give up.* But our response must always be defined by the truth of God's Word.

In 2 Corinthians 12, the apostle Paul was afflicted with something he referred to as a "thorn in [his] flesh." We do not know the nature of this affliction, but it clearly brought great torment into Paul's life. We can sense the deep emotion in his prayer for healing —"Three times I pleaded with the Lord to take it away from me" (2 Corinthians 12:8). Many people believe that this should have settled the issue. Paul prayed in faith (even pleaded), so God *must* automatically answer with healing. The problem is that prayers are not coins we insert into spiritual vending machines. The Lord answered the *repeated* prayers of Paul with the following principle: "'My grace is sufficient for you, for My power is made perfect in weakness'" (9).

This type of truth cuts against the grain of our normal thinking because weakness is despised in our modern culture. *But in God's Kingdom, weakness becomes a great commodity as it allows the Lord to demonstrate His grace and power through our brokenness.*

In grief and loss, we encounter levels of pain that seem destined to crush us. The rebuilding of our devastated ruins seems impossible when contrasted with our spiritual, physical and emotional weakness. But God's grace is always sufficient, and His power will strengthen us. We experience a profound identification with the heroes of Hebrews 11 as we personally discover the truth that was made real to "the great crowd of witnesses"—their "weakness was turned to strength" (Hebrews 11:34; 12:1).

The second tool that Sanballat uses to bring discouragement is revealed in the question: "'Will they *restore* their wall?'" (Nehemiah 4:2, emphasis added). I believe this thought is a challenge to compare the past to the present. Nehemiah knew these collapsed walls used to be strong and dignified, a visible demonstration of God's blessing in the Holy City. The disheartening suggestion is clear: Do you really think they can ever be *beautiful* again?

The enemy loves to flood devastated lives with this kind of negative thinking. Take, for example, a person who is fighting to rebuild her personal world after it has been smashed by alcohol or drug addiction. Standing knee-deep in rubble, her mind tries to tell her that her life will never be beautiful again. The pain is so great and the losses seem so final that she is robbed of the hope for any future recovery.

The historical framework of Nehemiah's time provides us with the scriptural response to this lie. As the Jews are trying to rebuild the temple, they are battling a pessimism produced by comparing the glory of Solomon's temple with their present ruin. The prophet, Haggai (a contemporary of Nehemiah's), speaks to the people, and his prophetic word rings out to us centuries later—"'"The glory of this present house will be greater than the glory of the former house," says the Lord Almighty. "And in this place I will grant peace . . ."'" (Haggai 2:9).

What an amazing word of encouragement to hurting people! *No matter how desperate the present damage may appear, God is able to bring us into peace and rest as He makes our lives more beautiful than they were before.*

In the aftermath of our daughter's death, my family struggled with the seeming impossibility of this truth. I will share more completely about this part of healing in chapter seven, but for the moment I can state unequivocally the following: *God is able, through His grace and power, to bring restoration and beauty to shattered lives in a way that transcends what was formerly experienced.*

The third part of Sanballat's discouraging attack is reflected in his question: "'Will they *offer* sacrifices?'" (Nehemiah 4:2, emphasis added).

If the Old Testament sacrifices offered from a pure heart were a reflection of true love and worship, then the accusing implication becomes crystal clear. The enemy wants to suggest we will never be able to love and worship the Lord in the way that we did before the loss occurred.

In personal relationships, the experience of walking with another through painful circumstances can actually make the relationship stronger than it was before. As my family and I faced the pain of our loss together, we discovered the Lord bonded us with a solidarity that can never be shattered. The same principle is true in our relationship with Christ. If our hearts remain open to Jesus and His Word, the broken ruins of our lives will be rebuilt as He leads us into new depths of love and worship.

The following two questions of Sanballat combine into one focus as he assaults the people with two negative accusations: Can they finish, *and* can they "'bring the stones back to life from those heaps of rubble—burned as they are?'" (Nehemiah 4:2).

The first bullet in his last round of discouraging attack is related to the possibility of *completion*. We've started the process, but what is the real chance of completing it? This question looked at closely also raises the issue of time: Can it be finished in a day?

The correct answer is yes *and* no. *Yes*, the Lord will always finish the rebuilding work He has begun (Philippians 1:6). *No*, He will not accomplish the final restoration overnight. Because healing takes time, the enemy is committed to produce *impatience* in our hearts so that we will walk away prematurely from the completion of God's finished work.

The second part of this last attack focuses on the very thing God desires to accomplish in His process of true healing. Can the burned stones from our past be a part of true restoration?

The Hebrew word for revive is *chayah*, and it means "to live" and "refresh." *Chayah* describes a restoration that allows a person to "enjoy life" again. The questions of discouragement at this juncture are really inverted prophetic barbs that unmask the lies seeking to rob us of hope. In fact, yes, God is able to use the most severely burned stones in His restoration of life, order and beauty. In the final fruit of the healing process, we are truly able to enjoy our lives again.

It was a year after my daughter's death that I began to struggle with the reality of these types of questions: Would I ever be able to experience the blessing of God? Would I ever be able to fully enjoy life and laugh again? Would I be able to rediscover a confident expectation for my future? Because of the Holy Spirit's healing ministry, the answer to all of these questions is a triumphant *yes!*

We see a testimony of this miraculous restoration in Nehemiah 8 after the walls have been completely rebuilt. The passage describes a dramatic scene involving Nehemiah the governor, Ezra the priest and scribe, and the Levites who are instructing the people. The people are listening with respect as Ezra stands on a high wooden platform reading the Word of God.

As Ezra blesses the people, they bow down and worship the Lord "with their faces to the ground" (8:6). As they continue to worship in response to God's Word, we are told they *all* begin to weep. What the leaders say next is astounding—"This day is sacred to the

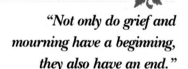

*"Not only do grief and mourning have a beginning, they also have an end."*

Lord your God. Do not mourn or weep . . . do not grieve, for the joy of the Lord is your strength'" (9-12).

This command establishes a most amazing principle: Not only do grief and mourning have a beginning, they also have an end.

David shares this same principle in the Psalms when he says, "You turned my wailing into dancing; You removed my sackcloth and clothed me with joy, that my heart may sing to You and not be silent. O Lord my God, I will give You thanks forever" (30:11-12).

In God's healing plan and process, there is always a definite conclusion. The weeping and sackcloth are replaced with dancing and joy as we are brought into a place of worship and gratitude.

I want to be very careful and sensitive in how I state this truth of the promised healing, so as not to imply that healing means forgetting the loved one. While enjoying my own healing, for example, I know I will *never* forget the memory of my cherished oldest daughter and the granddaughter I never got to embrace. In a prominent place in our home, we have a small collage of pictures (not a shrine) that honor René's memory. As I look at these photographs, there are still days when I shed tears in response to the wonderful memories that will forever be engraved in my heart, but *because* of God's grace, I have experienced an end to my grief. It wasn't something that I arrived at quickly, and it took four years before I felt that I had turned a corner; but I can move forward, *now*, into a bright restored future because the joy of the Lord gives me strength.

Yes, there is "a time to weep and a time to laugh, a time to mourn and a time to dance . . ." (Ecclesiastes 3:4). In the walk of grief, genuine healing cannot be rushed, and it doesn't happen overnight—but there is a conclusion. The deepest comfort and completed healing can be experienced, however, only as we understand and properly pursue the *process.*

Another question inserts itself into our discussion at this point: Why do some people find it difficult to arrive at the place of *completed* restoration and healing? I want to suggest that the attitudes of our hearts will either facilitate or sabotage God's work of healing. Our attitudes will do one thing or the other. The facilitating heart attitude that moves us towards complete healing is rooted in the understanding of covenant relationships.

## PRINCIPLES OF BIBLICAL COVENANT AND HUMAN SUFFERING

The way Christians respond to God in the experience of human suffering is directly related to their understanding of biblical covenant. In examining different covenants of the Bible, we discover that each one is an agreement expressed in three parts.

The first part of covenant is demonstrated with spoken *words* and *promises*. When God entered into covenant with Noah, for example, He promised never again to "'destroy all living creatures'" (Genesis 8:21).

A visible *sign* followed the spoken words to provide a continual reminder of the promises that were made. The sign for Noah and his family became the beautiful rainbow that appeared in the sky after the floodwaters subsided. God said to Noah, "'I have set my rainbow in the clouds,'" and "'it will be the sign of the covenant between me and the earth'" (9:13). We are reminded every time rain falls and a corresponding rainbow appears that God made certain promises thousands of years ago.

The last part of biblical covenant is ratification demonstrated by the *shedding of blood*. Although this may sound strange to the twenty-first century mind, it's a vital part of understanding the outworking of covenant relationships in the Bible. The Scriptures affirm that the life of a living creature is in its blood (Leviticus 17:11). The application of this truth implies that, once blood is shed, the promises of a covenant become binding and can never be broken.

In the biblical understanding, a covenant is both acknowledged and confirmed by the shedding of blood. God's affirming response to the sacrifices Noah made after the Genesis flood are best understood in connection with this third part of covenant. In the expression of promises, the giving of a visible sign and the shedding of blood, biblical covenant agreements were enacted.

These three parts of covenant also give us significant insight into the covenant of marriage. When a couple stands at the marriage altar, they are essentially making promises to one another. In 1968, I looked into the eyes of my bride and made lifetime vows. I told her that I would "have her and hold her" from that day forward—"for better, for worse, for richer, for poorer, in sickness and in health, to love and to cherish" until we were parted by death. And then I added for emphasis—"As God is my witness, I give you my promise."

Connie followed by making similar promises that concluded

with the reading of Scripture and the exchange of our marriage rings. Before I placed the ring on my wife's hand, the minister prayed the following prayer: "Bless, O Lord, this ring to be a *sign* of the *vows* by which this man and woman have *bound* themselves to each other, through Jesus Christ our Lord, amen."

In all cultures of the world, there are different ways of connecting promises with visible signs as couples enter into the marriage relationship. In the Old Testament, the shedding of blood was also a tangible part of the marriage covenant. If a woman's hymen was intact, first intercourse would generally produce the shedding of blood, providing a visible reminder of how binding the promises would be for a couple that had become one flesh.

The only way to sustain commitment during the intense crises encountered in marriage is to stay rooted in the covenant promises that were made. The day of my marriage was a beautiful, sunny, September day in the high 70s. My bride was beautiful and ravishing as we faced each other in the church that had been freshly cleaned and beautifully decorated. Standing in the midst of gorgeous flowers, everything seemed perfect in the sunny, blue sky of our world. I believe now that I understood the ramifications of the promises I made on that Saturday afternoon, but the reality of "for better, for worse" seemed remote to me at best. How could there ever be anything but "better" for a relationship being born in the middle of such perfect surroundings and circumstances?

Four months after our marriage ceremony, I got a more focused insight into the reality of the promises we had made. In January of the New Year, Connie and I were involved in a serious motor vehicle accident. Our lives had been spared, but my wife's leg was broken and our vehicle demolished. Several days later, we each came down with a case of stomach flu accompanied by high fevers. Lying side-by-side in our sickness, with a pail on each side of the bed, we turned and looked at one another. Connie's beautiful blonde hair looked very different than it had on the day of our wedding. I hadn't shaved, and neither of us had showered for two days. It wasn't pretty.

"We could die in this bed, and no one would find us for days," my wife groaned.

"I'll dump the pails," I moaned back, nodding in agreement with her observation as I struggled to the bathroom.

*In sickness and in health,* I thought. *I'm starting to get the picture.*

Marriages are filled with these kinds of ups and downs. Sometimes, the circumstances of life seem so positive that we have to pinch ourselves to make sure we're not dreaming. At other times, problems come crashing in with a force that seems to buckle our knees. The one constant reality that *never* changes is the promises we made in covenant.

I made a promise to my wife that I would *always* be there. If things are going smoothly, I will stand by her side. If life is shattered and falling apart, I will still be there to hold her. Continued perseverance in a covenant relationship will never be sustained by circumstances and feelings; it will be sustained only by commitment.

Nowhere is the relationship between covenant and marriage illustrated more powerfully than in the salvation provided by Jesus Christ. In the first administration of the Lord's Supper, Jesus makes the following statement: "'This cup is the new covenant in My blood, which is poured out for you'" (Luke 22:20). With the Cross becoming the ultimate *sign,* the three parts of covenant converge in the establishing of the glorious New Covenant that has

*"Continued perseverance in a covenant relationship will never be sustained by circumstances and feelings; it will be sustained only by commitment."*

reconciled us to Father God. The salvation that becomes ours at conversion is nothing less than being brought into a spiritual marriage that is based on covenant.

Paul speaks of marriage as a profound mystery that illustrates the relationship between Christ and the Church (Ephesians 5:32). Our heavenly Bridegroom declares with divine authority that He will never leave us or forsake us (Hebrews 13:5). The New Covenant means that Christ has become our heavenly Husband based on the foundation of *promises* He has made to us, and that these promises are eternally confirmed with the *sign* of the Cross and the sacrifice of His life's *blood*. The *promises*, the *sign* and the *blood* comprise the covenant.

With this background on covenant, we can now apply these principles to the experience of human suffering. When I am inundated with painful circumstances in my marriage relationship, I don't walk away. In sickness or health, for better, for worse, I promised to be there *with* and *for* my wife. *This kind of commitment does not make us superhuman husbands or wives; it's simply the outworking of biblical covenant.*

No one understood the spiritual application of this principle better than Job. My wife and I had the experience of losing *one* daughter. Job and his wife lost *all* of their children in the space of one day, accompanied by the minor (in comparison) exclamation point of complete financial ruin and destitution. It didn't seem that circumstances could be any worse, and then this godly man experienced a complete physical collapse as well.

It's hard to imagine greater pain being inserted into the life of any individual who was walking in a lifestyle of complete integrity and love relationship with his God. A logical response would have been to walk away from the relationship. "If this is how God is going to treat the ones that love Him the most, then find someone else to serve," one would have thought him to say. But Job understood the essence of covenant. After all of these cumulative losses, he asserted his trust with an amazing declaration: "'Shall we accept good from God, and not trouble?'" (Job 2:10).

The reality of covenant can't be illustrated more clearly or powerfully than the truth contained in Job's question. Jesus has brought me into marriage with Himself through the glorious New Covenant. He has promised never to leave me or forsake me.

On my side of the net, I must choose to love Him and serve Him no matter what happens in my life. Why? Because I share eternal covenant relationship with my spiritual Husband, and even the most terrible and devastating losses of life will not turn my heart away from Him. I *will* love Him when I am healed, and I *will* also love Him when difficult and painful, physical infirmities continue unresolved in my body.

I *will* love Him when everything is going smoothly in my family, and I *will* choose to love Him when I stand at the graveside of my daughter and granddaughter as their bodies are committed to the ground on a cold March day. My perseverance in love relationship with Jesus is not based on circumstances but based on a commitment that is rooted in the reality of the New Covenant.

I believe that our faith can be shipwrecked if we do not embrace the truth of biblical covenant and settle Job's question in the deepest recesses of our hearts. The love of Christ in our lives is unconditional and eternal. The apostle Paul confronts us with the reality of Christ's relentless love in Romans 8. He specifically mentions trouble, hardship, persecution, famine, nakedness and danger. He continues with death, life, angels, demons and all the present and future powers. His conclusion is that nothing "in all creation will be able to separate us from the love of God that is in Christ Jesus our Lord" (35-39).

*"My perseverance in love relationship with Jesus is not based on circumstances but based on a commitment that is rooted in the reality of the New Covenant."*

The question of Job provides a penetrating analysis into the theology that Paul communicates in Romans 8. When we experience devastating loss, we are confident that nothing can separate us from *His* love. His unconditional love is demonstrated in the covenant of the Cross and can never be shaken. The question for the believer is now connected with our commitment to covenant. *Nothing can separate us from His love, but will we allow pain and difficulty to separate Him from our love?*

The essence of true love is that it's expressed from one heart to another. Jesus will never withhold His love from me, but because of the losses of life, I can withhold my love from Him. "'Should we accept only good things from the hand of God and never anything bad?'" (Job 2:10, NLT).

The answer to that question will always be revealed through covenant principles. "For better, for worse, for richer, for poorer, in sickness and in health"—with my daughter present to hold or not—will I choose to love the Lord who has pledged His eternal love to me. As we surrender to God's process and covenant in the midst of shattering loss and pain, it's the deep response of our love that determines whether we will experience healing and fruitfulness or bitterness and barrenness.

Let's summarize the healing themes and principles of this chapter.

## SUMMARY

**God's healing process demands honesty on our part.** The experience of pain and loss will always include shock, confusion, anxiety, anger and sadness. If we ignore or deny these basic emotions, the healing process will short-circuit and break down in our lives.

**The depth of our pain will always be commensurate with the depth of love we had for that which was lost.** Deep love will always equal deep pain. The grief walk will be highly unpredictable and intensely personal, with no two people having exactly the same experience, even in the same loss.

**It's possible to receive emotional healing and to experience an end to grief.** This finished work is produced by God's grace imparted to our lives, and the enemy of our souls will strongly resist us because he understands the power of completed restoration.

**The principles of biblical covenant teach us about persevering commitment.** If we embrace this understanding of covenant, we will stay committed to Jesus, no matter what happens in the circumstances and losses of our lives.

**Time doesn't heal, but Jesus is a great Healer over time.** God is all-powerful and able to accomplish His will without effort in a moment of time, but He chooses to provide emotional healing in the form of a gradual process. This process of healing does not diminish His power in any way, but it does raise a question: Why *doesn't* God heal immediately? If He loves us as His beloved children, why not *shorten* the experience of grief and pain? This question points us to a profound principle and the theme of our next chapter.

# CHAPTER 4

# Understanding the Cross

### Principle 3:
### *True disciples take up their cross, follow Jesus and fellowship in His sufferings.*

The principle shared in this chapter will cut against the grain of some popular teachings currently circulating in the Church. Many leaders define God's blessing as the experience of "prosperity" in one dimension or another. This perspective often cites overflowing finances and immediate, automatic physical healing as the promises on which true faith must be built. Any financial difficulty or health problem is seen only as a temporary hurdle that separates the people who have *real* faith from those who don't.

To adherents of this popular instruction, suffering in the perfect will of God is understood as some outdated anomaly, and the reality of the Cross is anemically redefined as something that applies only to our initial salvation. Just recently in a student chapel service, for example, a guest speaker challenged the student body in the area of divine healing. At two different points of his message, the following phrase was repeated, "If you're not healed, it's because you don't believe the Word of God."

Any attempt to challenge this type of thinking is met most often by angry resistance and requires swimming against the strong current of Christian pop culture in this century. It's into this river that we now plunge with a desire to establish a true biblical understanding of the Cross.

## THE CROSS DEFINED AND UNDERSTOOD

The Greek word for Cross (*stauros*) comes from a verb that means, "to stand," and originally meant an upright pointed stake upon which a criminal was either tied or impaled. Death by crucifixion originated in the East, with Alexander the Great learning the procedure from the Persians. Rome adapted it from the Phoenicians and then perfected it as a form of capital punishment reserved for the most serious and heinous crimes against society. It was rare for a Roman citizen to be condemned to die in this way because the procedure was so repugnant to the Roman, Greek and Jewish minds.

Jesus willingly surrendered to the torture and shame of this kind of death and established the Cross as the central theme of New Testament revelation. One of the distinctive features of Christianity as contrasted with other world religions is that its central truth focuses on the humiliation of our Savior, the Son of God.

The Cross *is* most definitely the foundation of our salvation. Paul tells the Galatians "that the Cross of Christ alone can save" (Galatians 6:12, NLT). As Jesus spoke to Nicodemus about being born again, He declared, "'The Son of Man *must* be lifted up on a pole, so that everyone who believes in Me will have eternal life'" (John 3:14-15, NLT).

The preaching of the Cross as the exclusive doorway to salvation has *always* been an offensive message. Paul discusses this animosity with laser focus in his first letter to the Corinthians: "I know very well how foolish the message of the Cross sounds to those who are on the road to destruction. But we who are being saved recognize this message as the very power of God," yet "it is foolish to the Jews because they want a sign from heaven to prove it is true. And it is foolish to the Greeks because they believe only what agrees with their own wisdom. So when we preach that Christ was crucified, the Jews are offended, and the Gentiles say it's all nonsense" (1:18-23, NLT).

Nothing has changed in our century. When Jesus embraced the

Cross, He surrendered to a form of punishment that was reserved for the worst criminals. It was a painful *and* disgraceful way to die, meaning that any application of the Cross to our personal lives will always be connected with suffering and shame.

The way of the Cross will lead us into pathways of pain we would never choose on our own. North Americans especially resist a theology that involves suffering because we have defined true spirituality as pursuing paths that produce the *greatest* amount of pleasure and the *least* amount of pain. Anything that hurts must be avoided at any cost. Many church services are intentionally designed to anesthetize people by pumping them full of spiritual Novocain, enabling them to roll along in a pain-free bubble to the next Christian event.

*"I believe the Cross not only provides the foundation and door for salvation, but also defines the essence of the mature Christian life."*

I believe the Cross not only provides the foundation and door for salvation, but also defines the essence of the mature Christian life. Paul captures this truth perfectly at the end of his ministry as he articulates a personal vision statement: "I want to know Christ and the power of His resurrection and the fellowship of sharing in His sufferings, becoming like Him in His death, and so, somehow, to attain to the resurrection from the dead" (Philippians 3:10-11).

The goal of the Christian life, according to the apostle, is sharing in the *fellowship* of Christ's sufferings so we can be conformed to the image of our crucified Lord. As we discuss the experience of suffering, loss and pain in this chapter, we will examine the Cross by asking two questions: (1) What did the Cross mean to our Lord? (2) What does the Cross mean to followers of Christ? As we wrestle with these two questions, we will gain a deeper insight into the redemptive suffering discussed in chapter two.

## WHAT DID THE CROSS MEAN
## TO OUR LORD?

What did the Cross mean to Jesus in His humanity and personal ministry? It's emotionally overwhelming to discuss this question because there is a level of intensity in Christ's experience that we'll never be able to understand completely. The writer of Hebrews reminds us that we have not yet given our lives in the struggle against sin (12:4, NLT). Nevertheless, we are not only called by the Lord to embrace our personal cross, but also reminded that any refusal to do so demonstrates a basic unworthiness of being His true disciples (Matthew 10:38). We cannot respond to the challenge of biblical discipleship without considering the Cross from God's perspective.

**Life Emerges from Death**

The truth that *life emerges from death* provides us with the first clear window of revelation into seeing the Cross through the eyes of Christ. In the gospel of John, we're given the story of Jesus' entering the city of Jerusalem at Passover time. A large crowd greets and praises Him with the exclamation—"'Blessed is the King of Israel!'" (12:13). This is His triumphant entry into the Holy City, forcing the Pharisees to bitterly complain that "'the whole world has gone after Him'" (19).

After this incredible reception, Jesus begins to speak about His upcoming death. He uses the illustration of a seed falling into the ground and dying so that it will be able to produce an abundant harvest. The application of this teaching becomes clear when considered in the context of Christ's impending crucifixion.

Jesus is prophetically describing the Cross as He sets forth a basic principle of God's Kingdom: *Abundant life will grow from the soil of suffering and death.* This thought seems so overwhelming to Jesus that He pauses in midstream to pray to His heavenly Father. His prayer leads into a very personal confession: "'Now My heart is troubled, and what shall I say? "Father, save Me from this hour"? No, it was for this very reason I came to this hour. Father, glorify Your name!'" (John 12:27-28). There are three important truths that emerge in this amazing prayer.

*Firstly,* any cross that confronts us will cause our hearts to be troubled deeply. There can be no true Cross *without* the experience of intense emotional turmoil. For this reason, we must be careful never to cheapen the Cross by equating it with trivial discomfort. A flat tire on the way to work, a problem with my computer and scraping thick ice off my car windshield on a miserable New York winter day are a few examples of problems that should *not* be seen as crosses to be carried.

*Secondly,* it's possible to resist the work of the Cross. Jesus even states this possibility in connection with His own ministry as He formulates the question: "Should I ask the Father to save Me from this hour?"

Attempted resistance or escape can take many forms in the experience of personal suffering. It's impossible, of course, to reverse the traumatic events that bring pain and loss into our lives. As Job sits on the ash heap, he has no power to change circumstances back to the way they were before. The loss of his children, wealth and health were related to circumstances beyond his control. That is why grief and loss always bring the experience of *helplessness.* We are faced with shattering circumstances that we would never have chosen and find ourselves powerless to turn back the clock. It's possible, however, to cultivate a spirit of anger and bitterness as we attempt to escape through the process of denial and rebellion against God, thus resisting the Cross.

> *"God is never glorified in escape; rather, He is glorified through embracing perseverance."*

*Thirdly,* we are instructed that the Father is glorified by a decision to embrace the Cross with the corresponding pain that always accompanies it. Jesus is saying it loud and clear: God is never glorified in escape; rather, He is glorified through embracing perseverance.

The understanding of this prayer in John 12 provides us with a foundational principle for living in God's Kingdom. Life *and* fruitfulness are produced most powerfully through the experience of suffering. As with all Kingdom principles, this flies in the face of anything we would naturally choose. We don't want what makes us uncomfortable, let alone anything that brings pain. We want the "seed" of our lives to be safe and protected from injury.

The North American DNA has been defined from the beginning of our nation as "life, liberty and the pursuit of happiness." Anything that makes us uncomfortable must be avoided or resisted because true fulfillment and happiness can be experienced only in a pain-free environment, at least that's what we think. The biblical understanding of the Cross, on the contrary, takes us into a radically different mindset, turning our world upside down.

Jesus was completely consumed with the reality of choosing the Cross that was set before Him. Satan pulled out every weapon in his arsenal when he tempted Christ in the wilderness. There are certainly many profound levels of theological meaning in the temptation accounts, but one simple truth emerges immediately and clearly above all others: *Each temptation was offered as a shortcut, luring Christ to use His power for self-promotion while avoiding the path of self-denial, pain and suffering.*

The last horrifying temptation comes when Satan shows Christ all the kingdoms of the world *and* their glory. "'I will give it all to You,' he says, 'if You will kneel down and worship me'" (Matthew 4:9, NLT).

The response of Christ is incredible as He commands the Devil to leave His presence: "'Get out of here, Satan,'" Jesus told him, for the Scriptures say, ""you must worship the Lord your God and serve only Him""" (10, NLT).

In this severe rebuke of the Devil, Jesus gives us a powerful truth about worship. The deepest love and adoration we can give our Lord is always related to *choice*. When we embrace him in circumstances that involve suffering and sacrifice, we give Christ the highest form of worship *because* we choose to love and honor Him in our deepest pain.

Christ's victory over Satan in the wilderness becomes a foundational part of His public ministry. *Anything* that tries to turn Christ away from the pain and sacrifice of the Cross is viewed as demonic. Peter, His chosen disciple, is repulsed when Jesus speaks of how He will suffer many terrible things and then be killed. Peter presumes to correct Jesus with the reprimand, "'This will never happen to You!'" (Matthew 16:21-22, NLT).

The response of Jesus is startling. At one level, we could see that Jesus might give an affirmation to Peter because he's seeking to protect the Master that he loves and serves: "Thank you, Peter, for watching out for Me. I am so moved by your desire to protect Me and see it as proof of our deep friendship."

Instead, Jesus gives the most severe rebuke imaginable: "'Get away from Me, Satan! You are a dangerous trap to Me. You are seeing things merely from a human point of view, not from God's'" (23, NLT). Looking back on this poignant scene, we too are smitten with the sharp rebuke, but we must see what Jesus was dealing with (and teaching) in that moment.

We can never understand the Cross by building on our finite human understanding. Jesus perceives that Satan is trying to present a crooked, substitute plan through the influence of a close personal friend. *This attempt to turn our Lord from the path of pain is seen by Jesus as demonic diversion, not caring friendship.* Why? Is Jesus clinging to some kind of twisted, monastic masochism? Absolutely not!

Our Lord was simply refusing any option that would divert Him from the Cross that He had chosen before the foundation of the world. As He surrendered to the pathway of suffering, He was allowing the seed of His life to be planted in the ground through death.

*In making this earthly choice, Jesus was honoring and worshiping the Father, but also accomplishing the fruitful harvest of our eternal redemption.* In this act of ultimate worship, Christ chose the path of self-sacrifice, making it possible for *life to emerge from death.*

## Life Emerges from Isolation

A second truth that helps us see the Cross from God's perspective is that *life emerges from isolation.* This is an extremely difficult principle to wrestle with, but I have come to see it as a key to understanding the deeper meaning of the Cross.

One of the driving passions in the life of our Lord was to do only what would please His heavenly Father. Luke tells the fascinating story of how Jesus, as a young Boy, was left behind in Jerusalem after a visit to the temple at Passover time. Because of the large family group that was making the pilgrimage, His parents didn't miss Him at first. In fact, their 12-year-old Son was missing in action for three days before they retraced their steps and found Him in the temple amazing the religious experts with His wisdom.

Joseph and Mary were exasperated as they challenged their adolescent Boy: "'Son, why have You done this to us? Look, Your father and I have sought You anxiously.'" And He said to them, "'Why did you seek Me? Did you not know that I must be about My Father's business?' But they did not understand the statement that He spoke to them" (Luke 2:48-50, NKJV™).

At 12 years of age, Jesus was already clear about His vision and mission. He *must* be involved in His heavenly Father's business. The focus for every decision, word and action in His life would always be traced back to this fundamental question: Will this action please and honor My Father?

In one of His many intense confrontations with the Pharisees, He declares: "'I assure you, the Son can do nothing by Himself. He does only what He sees the Father doing'" (John 5:19, NLT).

Later, Jesus adds insult to injury as He looks eye-to-eye with the religious establishment of His day and says, "'Your approval or disapproval means nothing to Me because I know you don't have God's love within you'" (41, NLT).

This commitment to please the heavenly Father finds its ultimate fulfillment in the prayer of Jesus as He confronts the final reality of the Cross, first falling on His face to pray in a garden. Everything that was lost in the first garden, called Eden, is about to be reclaimed in this second garden, called Gethsemane. But this radical reclamation requires that a critical choice be made.

Each of the four Gospels records a moving account of what happens at this decisive turning point of history. Jesus is struggling with the pain He feels and begins "to be deeply distressed and troubled" (Mark 14:33). He seeks to share some of His pain with Peter, James and John as He cries out: "'My soul is overwhelmed with sorrow to the point of death'" (34).

*"Everything that was lost in the first garden, called Eden, is about to be reclaimed in this second garden, called Gethsemane."*

As He moves more deeply into the garden, He collapses to the ground in weakness as He prays, "'Abba, Father, everything is possible for You. Take this cup from Me. Yet not what I will, but what You will'" (36).

As we look back to this moment of critical choice, we realize the depth of our Lord's agony at this point can never be measured, but we know that the intensity level was so great "an angel from heaven appeared to Him and strengthened Him" (Luke 22:43). Yet even with the empowerment of direct angelic intervention, He agonized beyond our understanding. Luke gives us the following footnote to explain the intensity of His struggle: "And being in anguish, He prayed more earnestly, and His sweat was like drops of blood falling to the ground" (44).

The incredible conclusion we discover in the Gethsemane experience is that the clutches of life-threatening pain could not turn our Lord from embracing the Cross. It was *not* the horror of physical pain and torture that caused Jesus to shrink back momentarily from the "cup of suffering." *It was His knowledge and awareness of the highest price tag of all—isolation from the Father.*

As Jesus hung suspended between heaven and earth, He received the sin of the world into His holy body. All of my darkness, rebellion and depravity was absorbed into His pristine purity, making it possible for me to become "the righteousness of God" (2 Corinthians 5:21). To understand this spiritual reality and how it relates to isolation, we must examine the fruit of sin.

The Bible speaks clearly about the consequences of sin in Romans 6:23—"For the wages of sin is death, but the gift of God is eternal life in Christ Jesus our Lord." With every sinful thought, intention and action, we are earning a paycheck called death.

When we speak of death, we normally limit the scope of our definition to the casket at the front of a church—but the essence or core meaning of death is always *separation*. Physical death is the *separation* of our body from our spirit and soul, creating a great gulf between the one who has crossed over and the ones left behind.

Spiritual death is the *separation* of our soul and spirit from the Holy Spirit of God. That is why God warned Adam and Eve that at the *moment* of rebellion they would "surely die" (Genesis 2:17). Death and separation are the immediate wages of any sinful behavior. Spiritual, physical, emotional, relational and environmental death is the consequence of the cosmic, historical rebellion that occurred in Genesis 3.

One of the basic struggles facing modern man is a pervasive alienation experienced in all of his endeavors. We have been cursed by the wages of sin. The ability to *see* the goal while being thwarted from achieving it describes a pain all people experience. We encounter in these frustrating moments a microcosm of our eternal alienation outside of Christ.

But as the Cross is planted in history 2000 years ago, the curse is broken. A dynamic reversal is now possible because God offers the "gift" of eternal life.

In our human efforts, we work for the wages of sin which always produces death. In our faith, we freely receive a gift that can never be earned—a gift called eternal life. As death is essentially defined by separation, so life is contrasted to death by the experiences of *union* and connection. Our sin brings separation and alienation, but the gift of God imparts union and relationship.

For this reason, the term *eternal life* should never be narrowly defined simply in terms of duration—as "living forever." Living forever will be no blessing for those who have rejected the gift of salvation. Eternal life should always be understood in the context of a certain *quality* of life.

*"Our sin brings separation and alienation, but the gift of God imparts union and relationship."*

Eternal life is knowing the "'only true God and Jesus Christ, whom He has sent'" (John 17:3). This is why the New Testament uses the term *eternal life* only in connection with people who have received Christ's gift of salvation. In faith, we can have relationship with God, instead of isolation and death. It's critical to recognize that this divine exchange is made possible *only* by the Cross.

The "'Son of Man must be lifted up, that everyone who believes in Him may have eternal life'" (John 3:14-15). The reality of this exchange was what became an almost overwhelming burden to our Lord in Gethsemane. He understood through intense prayer and the deep agony of His soul what the *most* horrendous price tag of the Cross would be. It was not physical death (separation) that caused Him to shrink back momentarily, but the surety of spiritual death (separation) that would produce a break in His perfect relationship with Father God.

As Jesus is dying, He utters seven short statements that have attracted the attention of theologians and biblical commentators for centuries. The ultimate expression of anguish comes at about the ninth hour (3:00 p.m.) when Jesus cries in a loud voice, "'My God, My God, why have You forsaken Me?'" (Matthew 27:46).

As *my* sin is absorbed into *His* body, Jesus must pay the death consequences for my rebellion. Because a holy God cannot identify with sin, the Father turns away from His Son. Jesus becomes alienated from life-union with the Father as their fellowship is broken for the first time.

The entire angelic host surely shudders in horror as all creation groans. Our union of eternal life is being purchased through death and spiritual isolation. *As He receives my sin, Jesus hangs alone, forsaken by Father God—not to pay the wages of His rebellion but mine.* It's through death *and* isolation that John 3:16 is made into reality: "'For God so loved the world that He gave His one and only Son, that whoever believes in Him shall not perish but have eternal life.'"

The meaning of the Cross rests on the foundational principle that life emerges from death *and* isolation. *Our suffering is embraced by His suffering as our wounds are healed by His wounds.*

Through His own abandonment by God, the crucified Lord brings those who have been abandoned and isolated by sin to Father God. On the Cross of Calvary, Jesus lets Himself be pushed out of the world in a demonstration of surrendered power and ultimate weakness. It's through His pain and isolation that our healing and relationship with God are secured. Hallelujah!

## WHAT DOES THE CROSS MEAN TO FOLLOWERS OF CHRIST?

Having considered the meaning of the Cross to our Lord, we turn to the second question we are considering in this chapter: What does the Cross mean to followers of Christ? The answer begins with a challenge that Jesus brings to any who would follow Him. One example of this challenge is found in Matthew 10, the chapter where Jesus sends out His disciples to preach the Gospel.

After imparting His authority, Jesus gives detailed instructions to guide their ministries, including the warning about the persecution and resistance they will face. The prophetic picture that Christ paints about persecution is quite graphic. It will involve religious, political and family dynamics. Furthermore, He warns that even siblings and parents will betray their closest family members to their death.

I have tried to insert myself personally into this chapter. I have watched the Master do ministry in all of its facets. He has dealt with evil spirits, healed sickness and preached the Gospel of the Kingdom in power.

At this point in the biblical text, He has transferred His authority and given me the privilege of doing the same things in His name. I am about to be overwhelmed with excitement and joy until Jesus begins to communicate His divine footnotes.

He says I will be like a sheep among wolves and will experience trouble, resistance and even death as I follow Him into ministry (Matthew 10:11-22). He concludes with the solemn warning that "'all men will hate you because of Me.'" At this point, everything in my being begins to cry out, "What kind of deal is this?!"

Jesus confronts this question head-on so we can never say that His footnotes are in *fine print*. He says, "'A student is not above his teacher, nor a servant above his master. It is enough for the student to be like his teacher'" (24-25). Jesus is asking a fundamental question to all disciples of Christian history: Do you want to be like your Master? If the answer is yes, then you must walk in the path of suffering.

Jesus adds many other perspectives but concludes with a challenge to embrace the Cross—"'Anyone who does not take his cross and follow Me is not worthy of Me.

*"Do you want to be like your Master? If the answer is yes, then you must walk in the path of suffering."*

Whoever finds his life will lose it, and whoever loses his life for My sake will find it'" (38-39). His message is clear and powerful. If we do not embrace the Cross, we cannot be His disciples *and* we are not *worthy* to be His disciples.

When Jesus is making this application, He is not speaking only of our entrance into the Kingdom and our desire to be a witness for Him in the world. He is describing our ongoing daily walk with Father God. A disciple must be *like* his Teacher; this means we'll encounter suffering and pain we don't deserve. To lose our lives is to find them (i.e., *life emerges from death*).

These challenges are given as Jesus is commissioning His disciples, but He continues to build on this charge in His confrontation with Peter in Matthew 16, nearer the time when He faces His own Cross. In our earlier discussion, we have noted Christ sees attempted demonic interference when Peter suggests God would never allow Jesus to "suffer many things" (Matthew 16:21). It's important to pay close attention to the further response of our Lord, directed to *all* His disciples. He turns to the whole group and tells them, "'If anyone would come after Me, he must deny himself and take up his cross and follow Me'" (24).

There are some vital observations that must be noted in this passage of Scripture. Jesus not only embraces this prophetic word *personally*, but also applies it to *all* those who want to follow Him. He essentially looks at these twelve men and says, "Listen, boys, Peter is wrong. The pain awaiting me in Jerusalem is not optional. I must suffer these things. But this experience is not only for Me. It's also for you and all who will follow Me. *There is a destiny for each one of you, and it involves a cross.* If you are going to follow Me, you *must* deny yourselves in the embracing of that cross."

In the Matthew 10 discourse, Jesus has communicated that rejecting the Cross will make them *unworthy*. Now, He intensifies His counsel and makes it a command—"You *must* do this if you're going to follow Me."

Jesus is *not* suggesting that there is an easy road and a difficult one, and if you really want to impress the Father, choose path number two. *He is pointing to the Cross and the way of suffering and saying, "This is the mandatory path for any true disciple in My Kingdom."*

The choice that confronts every believer is not between easy and difficult. The choice is between *genuine* or *pseudo* discipleship. The essence of what I call the "new gospel" is that Jesus did all of the hard work to make it easy for me. Because of His pain, I am exempt from being hurt. I don't know where we found this distorted gospel, but it certainly wasn't in the teaching of Jesus.

The apostle Paul sets forth the implications of Christ's teaching in his epistles. In his letter to Rome, he stresses the reality of God's Fatherhood in the life of the believer. We are true sons and daughters of God, and by the Spirit "we cry, 'Abba, Father.'" The Holy Spirit testifies constantly to our spirits that we are His children (Romans 8:14-18).

Paul builds on this glorious truth with the exciting news that true sons and daughters have an inheritance. *Our inheritance is not silver, gold, lands or a stock portfolio. No, our inheritance is God Himself.* All the endless treasures of His infinite Person are given to us in this ultimate eternal inheritance.

What, according to Paul, do we have to do to receive this incredible inheritance? The grace of God has already purchased it for us through the blood of Christ, so there is nothing we can do to earn it. But he continues by telling us that following Jesus at times will lead us into the experience of pain and suffering. Paul focuses on this point. We will be glorified "if indeed we share in His sufferings in order that we may also share in His glory" (17).

The road that leads to our inheritance is not a smooth highway. Jesus has chosen to share *all* that belongs to Him. He shares His glory *and* His sufferings.

Some might respond and say, "If that's what discipleship is, forget it! No *future* glory could be worth suffering in the *present.*"

Paul anticipates this response and says in so many words, don't even think it, as he reminds us of eternal values and eternal rewards: "I consider that our present sufferings are not worth comparing with the glory that will be revealed in us" (18). *Just as no sin is so black or deep that it cannot be cleansed in the light of God's grace, no suffering is so great that it will not be overshadowed with the glory destined to liberate all creation.*

How can we know this for sure? Paul says that there can be no doubt because we have been given the first fruits of the Spirit (23). The Holy Spirit has been given as a down payment on the full inheritance that will be entrusted to us when we are received into the Eternal Kingdom. We will share forever in His glory if we share for a moment in His sufferings.

Paul states this truth from another perspective in his letter to the Philippians. In chapter three of this epistle, he is attempting to express in clear language what Christ means to him. After setting forth a most impressive résumé describing his training and qualifications, he compares his accomplishments to relationship with Christ (4-6). "Whatever was to my profit," he tells us, "I now consider loss for the sake of Christ" (7).

*"We will share forever in His glory if we share for a moment in His sufferings."*

Paul then begins to articulate the price tag that has been attached to his ministry. "I have lost all things" and "consider them rubbish that I might gain Christ" (8). The history of Paul's life bears out this testimony. He tells us in some detail about his losses in 2 Corinthians 11, and of course the letter to the Philippians is being written from a prison cell. He's saying in essence, "I have lost it all, and it means nothing." This is the testimony of the man who is about to face martyrdom.

A mindset like Paul's is repugnant to us, and we find it shocking and offensive. *How can anyone experience that kind of loss and pain and still maintain a testimony of confidence?* Paul gives us two answers.

Firstly, he can maintain his confident testimony because he possesses the reality that he is in Christ and has "the righteousness that comes from God" by faith (9). To know that we can stand in the presence of the Holy God and be covered by Christ's righteousness is worth paying any price. "I have been shipwrecked, beaten, imprisoned and will soon lose my head *but* the righteousness of Christ has been imparted to my spiritual account" is Paul's bold confession.

Secondly, Paul gives us an intensely personal life mission statement. All of his losses and pain have pressed him into deeper relationship with Christ. "I want to know Him and the power of His resurrection," he declares and then shares the insight that has produced this deep longing in his life. To know Christ intimately demands entering into "the fellowship of His sufferings" (Philippians 3:10). Paul is applying the Kingdom principle that he described in Romans 8 to his present situation: I can somehow "attain to the resurrection from the dead" if I become "like Him in His death." This is simply another way of saying that we will inherit His glory if we share in His sufferings.

The word that Paul uses to describe his relationship with suffering is of great importance. He uses the word *fellowship* that is the translation of the Greek word *koinonia*. This is the word that is used throughout the New Testament to describe intimate relationship, communion and even partnership. In Luke's writing, it describes the fellowship of the early church when they devoted themselves to "fellowship [*koinonia*], the breaking of bread and prayer" (Acts 2:42). When Paul is warning the Corinthians about being joined together with unbelievers he asks, "What fellowship [*koinonia*] can light have with darkness?" (2 Corinthians 6:14-17).

The apostle John uses *koinonia* to describe our communion with the Father and one another (1 John 1:3, 6-7). He links this *intimate* partnership and fellowship to "walking in the light as He is in the light."

Even a superficial word study of *koinonia* reveals Paul's heart in connection with the pain he has experienced in life and ministry. Paul is convinced that, if he's going to "know Christ and the power of His resurrection," then he must share in the "fellowship of His sufferings." Any deviation or shortcut that takes him away from embracing suffering is seen as a compromise of true discipleship.

*Taking up my cross is not something mystical, nor is it only saying no to my own will and desires.* It's nothing less than intimate fellowship with the very sufferings of Christ that increases my capacity to know Him and forms within me the image of the Master I love.

Peter's theology is perfectly consistent with the revelation given to Paul. In one of the post-resurrection appearances, Jesus prophesies to Peter, the man He is restoring, with the warning—"'When you are old you will stretch out your hands, and someone else will dress you and lead you where you do not want to go'" (John 21:17-23). John gives us the inside comment that Jesus is indicating the kind of death "by which Peter was going to glorify God."

Jesus then looks into Peter's eyes and says, "'Follow Me.'" Peter's first response is to point at the apostle John and say, "'Lord, what about him?'"

*"The core issue is not what happens to my brother or sister, but whether I will follow Him no matter what happens to me."*

Jesus counters with the possibility that He might choose a different plan for John, and says, "'What is that to you? You must follow Me.'"

This passage has much to teach us about *fellowship* with the sufferings of Christ. Jesus has designed a unique path for each of His disciples, and at times my road may seem to be more difficult than that of the person next to me. In such situations, I am tempted to say that it had better be the same or it's not fair. But Jesus responds and tells me not to *compare* my suffering with another's. The core issue is not what happens to my brother or sister, but whether I will follow Him no matter what happens to me.

We are not told specifically in John's Gospel about how Peter responds to this challenge, but the testimony of his life and ministry rings loud and clear. In his first epistle, he has a lot to say about suffering.

"Do not be surprised at the painful trial you are suffering, as though something strange were happening to you," he announces with authority and clarity (1 Peter 4:12-19). We *are* caught off guard when difficulty and pain intrude into our lives, but Peter is warning us not to see these as some *abnormal* experience. Instead, Peter tells us to rejoice that we are able to "participate in the sufferings of Christ," so that we "may be overjoyed when His glory is revealed."

Peter meshes his theology with Paul's teaching in Romans 8. There is always a close relationship between *suffering* and *glory. I must experience the preparation of suffering as I move towards embracing my eternal inheritance.*

In an earlier part of his epistle, Peter links this preparation with the concept of purification. He asserts that right now we are suffering "grief in all kinds of trials," but we can rejoice because our faith is being "refined by fire" (1 Peter 1:3-10). Peter is convinced that the experience of suffering and grief will result in "praise, glory and honor when Jesus is revealed."

We are then given a clear word of counsel on how to respond in the experience of suffering. Those who suffer "according to God's will should commit themselves to their faithful Creator" (4:19). This connects us with the definition of trust that we shared in chapter two. We are called to trust God in situations we might *never* understand, surrendering our *why* questions with a full confidence that He is always faithful.

The apostle John adds a powerful concluding point to this part of our discussion. In the final book of the New Testament, he receives a glorious revelation of Christ while a prisoner on the island of Patmos. As we noted in chapter one, it's important to see that this revelation of God's glory is given in a life-context of suffering. John is writing to the Seven Churches as a political prisoner where tradition tells us that the Roman authorities try to boil him in oil. Notice his words as he introduces himself: "I, John, your brother and companion in the suffering and Kingdom and patient endurance that are ours in Jesus" (Revelation 1:9-11).

That single statement gives a concise summary of all that we have been saying. John is giving us a powerful word picture in the form of a triangle—suffering, Kingdom and patient endurance. If we follow the Lord, we will experience *suffering.* John is careful to point out the circumstances of his *own* life at this point.

He continues with the promise of experiencing *Kingdom.* Suffering will never halt or hinder the ongoing establishment of God's Kingdom in my life, but instead leads me into a deeper submission to the King. Suffering keeps us in a place of dependence, which establishes more deeply the rule of Christ in our hearts.

Thirdly, John challenges us to *patient endurance*, the attitude that says we will never give up or turn away from the glorious King. The key phrase that binds all of these words together is that they "are ours in Jesus" (Revelation 1:9). John is stating it with such force. *Suffering should be expected because it's in Jesus.* If suffering is *patiently endured*, it will establish Christ's *Kingdom* in my life.

Wherever we turn in the New Testament, we see a consistent testimony in connection with suffering and the Cross. The teaching of Jesus, Paul, Peter and John confirms these truths over and over. Beyond those I have referenced, I have left untouched and unexplored other significant passages that would further strengthen this teaching. One glaring omission is the theology of suffering that we see in the book of Hebrews. On the foundation that we have laid, however, we can now begin to apply these principles in our next chapter.

## SUMMARY

**Life emerges from death**. It's a basic principle of God's Kingdom that the seed must fall into the ground and die to produce fruit. Jesus provides us with the perfect example of this principle in His own life and teaching.

As we follow in His steps, we are confronted with the challenge of a lifelong Cross. At times, this Cross may thrust great loss and pain into our personal lives, but through perseverance these experiences form us into Christ's image. As we embrace the way of the Cross, we model true discipleship to a hurting world.

**Life emerges from isolation**. Any true experience of the Cross involves the *feeling* of abandonment by God. Jesus experienced this in a way that we will never know because our sin was imparted into His body on the Cross. This spiritual impartation produced His cry of anguish quoted from Psalm 22:1—"My God, My God, why have You forsaken Me? Why are You so far from saving Me?"

In our walk with God, Jesus has promised that He will never leave or defraud us, but the experiences of pain and loss make us *feel* isolated *and* alone. We find it difficult to believe that God is there, or that He hears our prayer. In the intensity of these times, we experience a deep brokenness as waves of suffering sweep over us. The brokenness produced through the feeling of isolation releases the life of Christ through us to a hurting world. It is this biblical truth that we will attempt to develop more fully in our next chapter.

# CHAPTER 5

# Embracing the Cross

### *Principle 4:*
### *Healing and fruitfulness are experienced*
### *when we embrace the way of the Cross.*

I
t's one thing to understand what is required of us as true disciples; it's quite another thing to embrace the way of the Cross. We now begin the difficult *application* of these scriptural principles to the suffering that we experience in our personal lives.

I would like to begin by making three foundational observations. *First* of all, the Cross is the historical event that makes salvation possible. It's neither a mythological *nor an* allegorical concept. The Son of God actually entered into space-time history, limiting Himself to a physical body and humbling Himself as a servant.

In the experience of a criminal's death, Christ's blood provides our redemption. As I accept His act of supreme love with the empty hands of faith, my sin is cleansed and His righteousness imparted. The words of the apostle Paul speak across the centuries to us: "God saved you by His grace when you believed. And you can't take credit for this; it is a gift from God. Salvation is not a reward for the good things we have done, so none of us can boast about it. For we are God's masterpiece. He has created us anew in Christ Jesus, so we can do the good things He planned for us long ago" (Ephesians 2:8-10, NLT). *The essential declaration of these verses is that the fruit of abundant life has sprung from the soil of Christ's suffering, pain and death.*

*Secondly,* the application of the Cross means that we must deny ourselves. We have all been marked by the Fall in Genesis 3. One of the results of our universal condition is a pervasive selfishness where I seek what is best for me. Sin means that I put myself at the center of the universe and don't care what my actions will mean for my family, friends, neighbors or persons on the other side of the world. I want everything *my* way, and I don't care what the cost will be for someone else.

Jesus brings the challenge of His Cross to *my* selfish attitudes. "Do you want to follow Me?" He asks. "Then pick up your cross *daily* and *deny* yourself." I must choose daily what *Christ* wants, not what *I* want. We must be willing to lay down our lives for Him and others, and as true sons and daughters of the Cross, we must live in such a way as to please only Father God.

The *third* observation is the hardest to understand and part of the focus of this book. It is the answer to a question I eventually found working its way into my grief, as I wrote at the end of chapter one. Let's ask it again: Is it possible to be fruitful in times of horrendous loss and pain? The answer is a resounding *yes* if we embrace a genuine theology of the Cross.

As I carefully set forth these principles, I want to stress that they in no way alter the conclusions we drew in chapter two. There are *why* questions related to the death of my daughter and granddaughter that will never be resolved in *this* life. These questions must be surrendered in trust to God. The Cross doesn't explain our pain, but rather redeems it.

This is the piercing reality of Romans 8:28: "And we know that in all things God works for the good of those who love Him, who have been called according to His purpose." The definitive word in this verse is *all,* and it's important to note that Paul is *not* setting forth some random, magical promise. In the preceding verse, he has reminded us that the Holy Spirit "intercedes for the saints in accordance with God's will" (27). God Himself is praying for us constantly in the times of our deepest pain. *Selah*—pause and think about that!

The Holy Spirit is praying for me as He asks the Father to work the most distressing circumstances of my life for *good.* The word *good* has a very sharp focus when it's defined in the next verse. The *good* Paul is speaking about is that we are "predestined to be conformed to the likeness" of the Son of God (Romans 8:29). As we walk through the valley of the shadow of death, we are comforted with the reality that the Holy Spirit is interceding and asking the Father to mold us more fully into the image of Christ.

*"As we walk through the valley of the shadow of death, we are comforted with the reality that the Holy Spirit is interceding and asking the Father to mold us more fully into the image of Christ."*

Our most intense times of suffering place us in the very footsteps of our Lord as He chose the Cross. With this divine imitation in mind, I want to center our thoughts for a moment on a neglected and misunderstood experience of the Cross.

## PERSONAL ISOLATION
## IN TIMES OF DEEP SUFFERING

We have previously highlighted the experience of isolation in our Lord's death on the Cross. The Father turns away as our sin is received into Christ's body, causing Him to cry out in a loud voice, "'My God, My God, why have You forsaken Me?'" As I have walked through the dark valley of my personal loss, I have come to understand that any true application of the Cross must include experiencing the *feeling* of isolation and abandonment by God.

The reality of Christ's *continual* presence with us in all circumstances must be *adamantly* stated here. Jesus, when He is giving the Great Comission, reminds the twelve disciples (and us) that "'surely I am with you always, to the very end of the age'" (Matthew 28:20). In the book of Hebrews, we are challenged to learn contentment, with the reminder that "God has said, 'Never will I leave you, never will I forsake you'" (13:5).

Paul, of course, gives us the same definitive promise in his epistle to the Romans. He begins by asking the ultimate question: "Who shall separate us from the love of Christ?" The description of possible scenarios begins with persecution, famine, nakedness, danger and the sword as "we face death all day long" and "are considered as sheep to be slaughtered" (Romans 8:35-39).

He continues with the realities of death, angels, demons and other powers related to present *and* future. The conclusion and eternal answer is that nothing "in all creation will be able to separate us from the love of God that is in Christ Jesus our Lord."

These Scriptures give us clear *and* conclusive testimony that the presence of our God is always with us. This *fact* is what creates such a great tension of faith in times of personal suffering.

In the months immediately after the death of our girls, I *felt* abandoned by God as I struggled with the *why* questions and cried out for His help. My experience was that the heavens were closed and God was silent. It seemed as though the Lord had taken a vacation from the Cline family. "Where are You, God?" I would moan in my times of debilitating anguish, as the full impact of King David's words began to pierce my soul: "My God, my God, why have You forsaken me? Why are You so far from saving me, so far from the words of my groaning? O my God, I cry out by day, but You do not answer, by night, and am not silent" (Psalm 22:1-2). I deeply identified with these prophetic words of the psalmist because they seemed to describe my own personal Calvary.

*I too was praying day and night, yet Christ had seemed to have moved to another galaxy.* I discovered other Psalms that seemed to have been written with my pain in mind: "How long, O Lord? Will You forget me forever? How long will You hide Your face from me? How long must I wrestle with my thoughts and every day have sorrow in my heart? How long will my enemy triumph over me?" (Psalm 13:1-2). These questions not only haunted me, but also for a time seemed to *define* the spiritual reality of my life. "I know You will never forsake me," I said to the Lord one day, "but I'm able to accept this truth only by naked faith."

Why was God so distant and silent in my life? One friend suggested I was thrashing around in a metal barrel of pain. God *was* speaking all the time, my friend assured me, but I couldn't hear Him because of the screaming echoes of my own anguish. I felt there was a measure of truth in that assessment, but God used another passage of Scripture, Psalm 42, to give me a clearer understanding of what was happening to me in my personal grief.

## The Feeling of Isolation and a Sense of Abandonment

Psalm 42 begins with the most intense expression of spiritual desire found anywhere in the Bible: "As the deer pants for streams of water, so my soul pants for You, O God. My soul thirsts for God, for the living God. When can I go and meet with God?" (1-2). It's hard to imagine a deeper longing for the presence of God than what is communicated in this passage. We're hearing the cry of one who is intensely thirsty for intimacy with the Lord. It seems fair to assume that God would come running to meet the cry of this panting soul. "Give me God or else I die," seems to be the essence of this prayer expressed in the words of beautiful poetry.

The psalmist continues with an incredible statement that seems inconsistent with the intense longing of his prayer: "My tears have been my food day and night, while men say to me all day long, 'Where is your God?'" (3). It's important not to miss the poetic irony of the psalmist's experience. He has just poured out his heart telling us how *thirsty* he is for God. Has this longing been met?

It appears not. The psalmist, in fact, is drinking, but it's the cup of his own tears. Day and night, he's weeping in the experience of *isolation* where God seems unwilling to show up.

I feel constrained at this point to mention briefly the concept of *defrauding.* I've counseled many couples in dating/courting relationships on how careful they must be never to defraud the other person. I define defrauding in the following way: We defraud someone when we stir desires in them that we have no intention of meeting or cannot meet and be true to the standard of God's Word. I always stress that God defrauds no one. He will never stir desires in our hearts that He will not meet in consistency with His holy nature.

In Psalm 42, the sons of Korah are describing desires that have been stirred by God. Left to ourselves, we'll not *normally* thirst for God like a deer panting for streams of water. It's the Person of the Holy Spirit that produces deep longing in the place of coldness and indifference. Why, then, is the psalmist experiencing spiritual *isolation*, comforted only by the memory of the way things used to be when he went to the house of God? (4).

Our answer is found later in the Psalm: "deep calls to deep in the roar of your waterfalls; all your waves and breakers have swept over me" (7). In this beautiful Hebrew poem, we've been given a most precious truth.

The waterfalls represent the stirrings of God in our hearts as He creates deep longing for His presence. The infinite deep in God calls out to the finite deep in me with the question—"Do you want more of Me?"

*"Just as breakers and waves wash the beach clean, so God uses brokenness to wash me clean from hindrances that would keep me from a deeper relationship with Him."*

"Yes," I respond, "I want You as the thirsty deer pants for water."

God then begins the process of spiritual preparation as His "breakers" and "waves" begin to sweep over me. For God to give me the desires that He is stirring in my heart requires a greater brokenness to happen in me. This brokenness is painful and may bring tears and loss, but God is not defrauding me.

Instead, He is working deeply within my heart to increase my spiritual capacity. Just as breakers and waves wash the beach clean, so God uses brokenness to wash me clean from hindrances that would keep me from a deeper relationship with Him. The psalmist has come to understand this at the end of the Psalm as he declares,

"By day the Lord directs His love, at night His song is with me—a prayer to the God of my life" (42:8).

Have you ever been comforted by a "song in the night"—a song that has become a prayer expressing the longing of your heart for God, a prayer that He stirs within you so that He can answer it at a profound level in your life? That is His *deep* calling to your *deep*, and your *deep* calling to His *deep*. It is His love washing over your wounded soul as it awakens your spirit to hope.

The conclusion of this Psalm confirms that God's love is ever present and He will never defraud us, but in the experience of pain and catastrophic loss we will encounter the *feeling of isolation* and a *sense of abandonment*. The suffering that we walk through will bring tears, as the shriek of emotional pain makes it difficult to hear His voice clearly. As we continue in faith to embrace the reality that His presence is *always* there, we'll experience deeper relationship with the Lord and be formed more perfectly into His likeness.

The principle of this chapter is that *healing and fruitfulness are experienced when we embrace the way of the Cross.* Let's look together at a few practical applications of what this really means.

## THE REDEMPTIVE FRUITS OF THE CROSS

Although the full outworking of these fruits is presented in the next two chapters, we will lay the foundation for their future development here. It's at this point we turn a corner in our walk through the valley of the shadow of death. God's grace is able to bring powerful healing *and* redemption, so grief and pain are *not* the final conclusion of anyone's story. Jesus states it so concisely in His Sermon on the Mount: "'Blessed are those who mourn, for they shall be comforted'" (Matthew 5:4).

### A Deeper Intimacy with God

The *first* fruit of new life for me was experienced in my personal relationship with God. Admittedly, I would never have anticipated how it would come to me—through suffering. When things are going smoothly, we give thanks to God. No one of us would ever think, *God, things are just too good right now. Please give me a heavy dose of pain and suffering.* The Scriptures *do* warn us, however, how easy it is to take God for granted.

Moses highlights this danger in the book of Deuteronomy. God will be bringing the people into a good and fruitful land. It's a place of blessing and abundance, the kind of life we dream about. Fruitfulness without pain—*yes!* But Moses challenges the people that it is the time to be careful. He cautions, "'Beware that in your plenty you do not forget the Lord your God . . .'" (8:11, NLT).

When all of the wheels fall off our lives, we're constrained to surrender to God in a more complete way. I walked in *real* intimacy with Jesus before the devastating losses of 1996. *After the funeral, however, I was able to see my daily need in a way that brought me into even deeper relationship.*

I have come to realize I don't need Jesus like my car needs gasoline. Without gas my car doesn't *function,* but it's still an automobile. In the valley of the shadow of death, I discovered that I need the Lord like my body needs oxygen. Without Him, I die. The words of Christ are now permanently engraved on my heart—that "'apart from Me you can do nothing'" (John 15:5).

## A Deeper Understanding of the Importance of Relationships with Family and Friends

The *second* fruit of new life was birthed in a deeper union with my family and friends. My marriage relationship has been forever strengthened. In the early days of my grief, I remember looking at Connie and saying, "I don't have anything to give you, but I will cling to you in my pain." Our understanding of covenant took deeper root as we embraced the reality that nothing but our own physical death could separate us. Our relationship was undergirded by the discovery that, if we survived this, then we could survive anything.

The same has also been true with my daughters, grandchildren and friends. *I cherish each moment with my loved ones and receive every hour as a special blessing from the hand of God.* Life is brief, fragile and uncertain which explains why Moses prays, "Teach us to number our days aright, that we might gain a heart of wisdom" (Psalm 90:12). The great prophet understood the urgency of this principle because our days "quickly pass, and we fly away" (10).

Every moment spent with family and friends should be redeemed as a valuable gift that might never be experienced again. The last moments on earth that I had with my oldest daughter were spent sitting side-by-side at the airport. She sat between her mom and me as we talked about the incredible future that was ahead for her. It was late morning on a Saturday, and I was supposed to be at a college basketball game. I had been given courtside tickets to Syracuse playing Notre Dame and had greatly looked forward to going. My daughter had pleaded with me to go. "Dad," she said, "Mom can take me to the airport. You love to watch Syracuse play. Please go."

I had vacillated back and forth but decided to give the tickets away and to accompany my daughter to the airport. I'll be eternally grateful for that decision and will forever cherish the hour I sat on a blue plastic seat at the Greater Rochester International Airport with my daughter's head on my shoulder. It was the gift of a precious moment that would never again be duplicated.

I want to be clear—I have *always* understood the importance of family time. I have stressed this principle to my students in the 30-plus years I have taught *Marriage and Family* at Elim. But pain and loss have a way of sharpening our spiritual vision, allowing us to see spiritual realities in a way we've never seen them before. I've come to understand the testimony of Job when he declares, "'My ears had heard of You but now my eyes have seen You'" (42:5).

### An Ability to Reconcile Faith with Unanswered Prayer

The *third* area of fruitfulness produced in my personal pain is a truth that provides a solid anchor in times of suffering. Simply stated it's the *ability to reconcile true faith with unanswered prayer.* Just looking at that statement on paper plunges us into deep and treacherous waters. I am more than familiar with the standard Christian clichés like God *does* answer every prayer. He says *yes* to some requests and *no* to others. Others claim that God didn't answer because *faith* wasn't strong enough or there was *sin* in the person's life or the *motives* were wrong. The variations are many and become cruel in their application as they are thoughtlessly spit out of the mouths of well-meaning people.

All of the clichés are compact and neat but not very helpful to someone struggling in the trenches of personal pain and loss. What about the wife who dies after being diagnosed with terminal cancer? The family reaches out to God in faith, seeking possible medical solutions, but always seeing prayer as the *key* to releasing healing, even traveling many miles to receive prayers from healing evangelists. Or the family that prays *earnestly* about their son's failing marriage. As they cry out to God for His intervention, they are confident that He is able to work miracles. A prayer chain of many watches with heavy hearts as the marriage dissolves and the daughter-in-law descends into mental and emotional hell.

**"All of the clichés are compact and neat but not very helpful to someone struggling in the trenches of personal pain and loss."**

I have a list of 23 friends, all of whom have experienced what seems on the surface to be a premature death, even after concerted and intense prayers ascended to the heavens for their healing. Some of those on this list were leaders who were touching the lives of many thousands of people. In these crisis situations, people have believed with all their hearts that God would do something miraculous and dramatic. Does Christ sit on His heavenly throne and say *yes* to some and *no* to others based upon His mood at the moment? Did no one have enough faith? Was there sin hidden in everyone's life? Was everyone praying with wrong motives? Let's attempt to address these questions.

We can never fully comprehend the *power* of prayer. Prayer is essentially defined as *communion* with God, where we experience two-way *communication* and are *changed* in the process. It's an often used and absolutely true saying that "prayer changes things." *Prayer is not some purely meditative spiritual exercise that takes place inside my own head, but it's relationship with the living God who hears and acts.*

These truths are precisely why unanswered prayer provides such a point of tension in connection with our faith. One of the prayers that my wife and I continually offered to God, for example, was for the safety and protection of our children. From the moment they were born, we asked God to watch over their lives spiritually, emotionally and physically. God answered our prayers, and through the years we became more and more convinced of the reality of Psalm 91:9-13, including the promise: "For He will command His angels concerning you to guard you in all your ways; they will lift you up in their hands so that you will not strike your foot against a stone."

In 1996, the shattering pain of our loss challenged the truths that we held so deeply in our hearts. As we felt our spiritual foundations shake, we were pressed more deeply into our relationship with God. Our Lord in His infinite faithfulness led us back to four cornerstone truths that ultimately reconciled faith and loss with our prayers.

**We pray to our loving Father.** *In many teachings I've heard on prayer, God simply becomes a glorified vending machine.* In this type of understanding, my prayer of faith becomes the dollar bill I insert in the slot to receive my candy bar. If I put in more than the designated amount, I even get change back! The apostle John seems to suggest that kind of interchange with this invitation: "'. . . Ask Me for anything in My name, and I will do it'" (John 14:14).

The extended teaching that Jesus gives about prayer is always pointing us to Father God. Christ came to reveal the Father and provide the way of access to Him. When you pray, He said, don't babble on and on as people of other religions do implying that our prayers will not be answered because we say the same thing over and over again. Instead, Jesus says, we should pray like this—"'Our Father in heaven . . .'" (Matthew 6:7-9).

We pray not from a mechanical spiritual formula. No, we pray to a Father with whom we share spiritual relationship. A true father will always be tuned in to what *his* children really need. If we know how to give good gifts to our children, "'how much more will your Father in heaven give good gifts to those who ask Him!'" (7:11). When we read such a verse, we immediately begin to think of the things that we want—a new car, a new house, the latest phone or other electronic component, a wife, husband, boyfriend or girlfriend, and the list goes on and on.

If we let Scripture interpret Scripture, we find Jesus helping us with a definition of what the "good gift" really looks like. In Luke's Gospel, we hear our Master's extended statement: "'If you sinful people know how to give good gifts to your children, how much more will your heavenly Father give the Holy Spirit to those who ask Him'" (11:13, NLT). The ultimate gift of God in prayer is not a material possession nor even a human being, but the *infinite* Person of the Holy Spirit. God's ultimate purpose in prayer is not about giving things; He wants to give us Himself.

In the most shattering circumstances of life when I have *not* received what I prayed for, I am promised the presence of the Holy Spirit who will never leave me. He comes as my Comforter and imparts the deep assurance that, even though I don't understand, my Father is in *control*.

*"God's ultimate purpose in prayer is not about giving things; He wants to give us Himself."*

**We pray to our omnipotent King.** This issue of control brings us to this *second* truth. When Paul speaks of the purpose in our eternal inheritance, he is certain we serve a God who "works out everything in conformity with the purpose of His will" (Ephesians 1:11).

When we speak of power in prayer, we have to recognize that this power finds its resting place in God. This presents a problem with my self-will and brings me back to the Cross because, if God has the power, then I lose control. We are justifiably concerned when we become aware of a great amount of power residing in one person because we recognize the possibility of abuse. That is precisely why Jesus begins with the invitation to pray to a loving spiritual *Father* who will never misuse His power and take advantage of us. *The amazing truth in our second point is that prayer enables us to draw on the unlimited power of God.*

Our prayers are in many ways like a spiritual blank check that Jesus puts in our hands, inviting us to fill in whatever amount we want: "'. . . I tell you the truth, my Father will give you whatever you ask in My name'" (John 16:23). It's most important to remember, however, that a check has a routing number on the lower left corner of the printed document. If you are giving a check over the phone, the financial representative will immediately ask for the routing number, ensuring that the check will move through channels and receive payment.

In our prayers to the Father, there is also a routing number. John actually gives us this spiritual number in his first epistle when he says, "This is the confidence we have in approaching God: that if we ask anything according to His will, He hears us. And if we know that He hears us—whatever we ask—we know that we have what we asked of Him" (5:14-15). John has imparted a most vital truth with these words. God will exercise His power only in connection with the routing number of His will.

Furthermore, *God's Fatherhood gives integrity to His actions, and His omnipotence gives focus.* Even the most painful things that come smashing into our lives are not occurring by random chance. These combined truths are intended to give us confidence in our prayer life: The awesome *power* of God will always be exercised in harmony with His Father's *love.*

**We pray to our omniscient Lord.** This, *third* truth will assist us in grappling with the issue of unanswered prayer by revealing one of the most precious truths of Scripture—that God is all-knowing.

The computer information highway has revealed to us how much

*"It's impossible for God to learn anything because He already knows everything."*

knowledge we'll never know in just the natural realm. Far beyond what man or computers know, our God possesses an all-inclusive, entirely retentive, instantaneous and pure knowledge of every-

thing there is, or was, or will be. It's impossible for God to learn anything because He already knows everything.

Jesus clearly had this truth in mind when He warned against vain repetition in prayer. We don't have to repeat a phrase over and over because our Father knows exactly what we need even before we ask Him (Matthew 7:8). The plain truth is that many times I don't understand what I really *need.* I know what I *want,* but that is a very different thing. *A very basic counseling principle tells me that, if what I want is not what I need, then what I get will never be enough.* I am so grateful for a spiritual Father who is committed to give me what I need.

Nothing would frighten me more than the ability to ask God for anything and have it granted. The reason that kind of authority would be horrifying is that I just don't *know* enough. Even with the help of God's wisdom, I can't completely see the future. *Pride demands,* "Lord, I know everything I need to know, so give me all that I pray for." *Humility surrenders* with the conviction that "Father knows best" because His omniscience sees all the contingencies I miss with my finite limitations.

**All prayer finds its final answer in God's eternal promises.** The writer of Hebrews gives us this *fourth* piece of understanding that reconciles the tension between confident faith and unanswered prayer. In the end, *all* prayer in accordance with God's will *is answered,* but not always in *this* life. In Hebrews 11, we're given an outline of the great heroes of faith. As we discussed in a previous chapter, these men and women were the ones "who conquered kingdoms, administered justice and gained what was promised" and now surround us as a "great cloud of witnesses" (Hebrews 11:33; 12:1).

But notice the startling revelation that comes through two separate statements in this great faith chapter. The writer informs us that "all these people were still living in faith when they died. They did not receive the things promised; they only saw them from a distance. And they admitted that they were aliens and strangers on earth" (13). Pause for a moment and consider this shocking statement: They did not receive the promise.

So that there can be no misunderstanding, the writer returns to this theme at the end of the same chapter: "These were all commended for their faith, yet none of them received what had been promised" (39). In much of the current teaching on faith, there is a strong emphasis on the unseen becoming reality. If we do not see the visible substance of the things that we hoped for, then it cannot be true faith. But our heroes in the words of Scripture did not always receive the promises in their earthly lifetimes.

Abraham's experience is a clear case in point. The *entire* land was promised to him, but the only portion he ever owned in this life was the plot he purchased to bury the love of his life, Sarah. The problem becomes even more complicated with the seeming contradiction found within Hebrews 11. Verse 33 states that they "gained what was promised," and verse 39 says that they didn't.

The key to resolving this problem is found in the phrase, "from a distance" (13). Because the promises of God are eternal, they can find their fulfillment in future generations *and* the Eternal Kingdom. This truth can be frustrating to many because we sometimes live as if *present* reality is all that there is.

As a young man, I was especially impatient with this concept of future fulfillment. If truth couldn't be apprehended in the "here and now," I didn't want to hear about it. *I have now come to understand that present reality is only a momentary shadow and that we are passing through this life as aliens and strangers.* This world is *neither* my true nor my final home, and because I serve the eternal God, His promises *and* answers extend far beyond the limits of my short physical existence.

It's within these four truths about prayer that we discover the last application of the Cross to personal pain and loss. I prayed consistently (throughout her life) for the protection of my daughter, and hundreds of Christians were praying for healing and deliverance at the moment of her death. At one level, I could say, "Case closed." God *didn't answer* the prayers of His people. But if I process my daughter's death in light of these four truths another answer emerges.

I begin with the understanding that I pray to a loving Father *and* the all-powerful King. Because I *trust* in His love, I can *surrender* to His power with the knowledge that René's death was *not* outside of God's control. It was not random chance or the power of the Devil that initiated the events of March 8, 1996. My heavenly Father was at work in these circumstances. I personally would have never chosen the final outcome of our personal Black Friday. I wanted my daughter to live a *long* life. After the funeral, this feeling intensified. One person came up to me within days of the interment and said, "You're going to be such an inspiration to so many people." Inwardly, I shrieked in anguish. If I could have answered honestly, my response would have sounded something like this—"Shut up! I don't want to be an inspiring example for anyone. I just want my girls back!"

My *will* would *never* have chosen the outcome of that dreadful Friday evening, and therein is the critical problem: I am afflicted with finite and flawed knowledge. I don't know the future and can't predict with certainty what will happen tomorrow. James targets this very issue when he asks, "How do you know what will happen tomorrow?" (4:13). He counsels us that our attitude should always be, "'If it is the Lord's will, we will live and do this or that'" (15). Otherwise, we are boasting about our own plans, and "all such boasting is evil" (16).

My limitation in the area of knowledge means that I need the

Lord to direct my future and interpret my present. God's omniscience challenges me to take yet another step in my relationship with Him. I'm asked to trust not only His Father's heart and power, but also His perfect knowledge as I am again confronted with the reality of the Cross.

I can fight the Holy Spirit for years with angry resistance as I refuse to yield my will. Or I can surrender with the Gethsemane prayer of Jesus: "'My Father, if it is possible, may this cup be taken from Me. Yet not as I will, but as You will'" (Matthew 26:39).

*"My limitation in the area of knowledge means that I need the Lord to direct my future and interpret my present."*

Because many of our prayers find their final fulfillment in God's eternal promises, I have come to believe that God did answer my prayers for the protection of my daughter. If protection applies only to this life, then God defrauded me—but if His promises are *eternal*, then they extend beyond the brief shadow of my temporal existence.

The Scripture makes the declaration that "man is destined to die once" (Hebrews 9:27). This appointment with death is something that awaits each human being. My generation (the baby boomers) doesn't really believe that. Many of my contemporaries who are outside of Christ act as though they will be able to live forever because of diet, exercise and medicine. They are mistaken because death is a journey that each must take.

My daughter, René, took her journey earlier than *anyone* expected, but God did protect her from the day of her birth to her final breath on March 8, 1996. He then protected her in death's transition as she was received into the Father's presence, and He will protect her now for all eternity. My prayers *have* been answered—here *and* there—as she finds herself eternally safe in the arms of the One who loves her completely and perfectly. With these conclusions stated, let's summarize the content of this chapter.

## SUMMARY

**The redemptive fruits of the Cross are demonstrated through finding deeper relationship with God and others**. Grief and loss are not the *final* conclusion of anyone's personal story, because for every cross there is a resurrection.

In the experience of pain, our spiritual vision is sharpened, enabling us to see spiritual reality with greater clarity than ever before. This is especially evidenced in developing a deeper relationship with God, accompanied by a desire to redeem the time in all of our personal relationships.

**In the embracing of the Cross, we are able to reconcile the prayers of faith with the appearance of unanswered prayer.** This important reconciliation takes place as we encounter more fully the Person to whom we pray. In the personhood of God, we find a loving Father, the all-powerful King and the all-knowing Counselor.

In *loving* the Father, we are able to *trust* the King with the awareness that He has our best interest at heart. In painful turbulent circumstances that we would never have chosen, we yield to His greater wisdom and knowledge. Although we may never fully understand why certain things have happened in this life, we know that final answers will be revealed in the Eternal Kingdom.

We have started to consider in this chapter the fruitfulness and healing that can be experienced in times of suffering, pain and anguish. Let's expand and develop our discovery by looking at another powerful principle in the next chapter.

# CHAPTER 6

# Giving out of Pain

### *Principle 5:*
### *Healing and fruitfulness are experienced*
### *when we give to others out of our pain.*

T his chapter is built on a foundational biblical truth: *Genuine transformation is always made complete through serving others.* In his letter to the Ephesians, Paul gives a clear and concise summary of how this principle is demonstrated in the life of the believer. I want us to see how it works specifically in the life of the suffering believer.

After giving a comprehensive theological presentation of the salvation that is provided in Christ, in the later chapters of Ephesians, Paul changes his emphasis to practical applications of *how* these sublime principles are lived out in daily life.

Christians long for the *deep* truths of God's Word and sometimes assume that these revelations will be mystical and difficult to comprehend. Offer a Bible study on finances, and 20 people may show up. Offer a study that will reveal the identity of the Antichrist and the beasts of Revelation, and 200 may come. We are obsessed and fascinated by the miraculous and spectacular.

When Paul gives his application of *deep* truth, however, it's always intensely practical. If you're a husband, how do you love your wife? If you're a parent, how do you treat your children? How do you treat your brother or sister in Christ? Do you walk in kindness, compassion and love, and do you forgive the people who have wounded you? These are all examples of the *deep* spiritual truths that Paul teaches in his epistles.

In Ephesians 4, he speaks directly about the principle of transformation expressed through servanthood. Let's examine his systematic progression as he addresses a brother who used to be a thief. "He who has been stealing must steal no longer . . ." is the opening challenge Paul brings (28). He *doesn't* say let's have a deliverance service to deal with the thief. In plain English, he gives a command: "Stop it! You used to make your living by theft. Cut it out of your life because a Christian doesn't live by that code. Don't steal anymore."

Many times, we stop with that preliminary understanding of transformation and define the Christian life in the negative—by what we *don't* do. We no longer steal, so we must be changed. But Paul continues with his practical exhortation in the positive: He "must work, doing something useful with his own hands" (28).

It's not enough to stop stealing. God wants to change someone who is a *taker* into a *worker*. We take all the energy and planning that we put into stealing, and we pour it into a job. This is certainly significant change, but it is still not complete transformation and wholeness—not until we become fruitful in blessing others.

The reason that we work is not just to provide for our own need, but also that we "may have something to share with those in need" (28). Notice the miraculous progression of complete transformation—yes, even when recovering from grief!

> *"It's through serving others that we experience full transformation."*

God's grace is demonstrated most powerfully by changing a *taker* into a *giver*. Working hard to provide only for my own needs can be selfish and self-centered. Many people understand the principle of hard work, but if my efforts are focused only on myself, I am still missing the complete cycle of change God desires to bring. It's through serving others that we experience full transformation.

This is a most difficult principle to implement in the experience of serious loss. When pain comes smashing into our lives, we desire to separate ourselves from other people. It's a natural tendency to retreat into our private world of personal pain and build walls of emotional protection. If someone has just experienced a divorce, for example, it can be excruciating to be invited into the home of a married couple who are holding hands and behaving as ones who are deeply in love. In this and other situations, there is a certain amount of healthy isolation that *needs* to occur when we are walking through the early stage of the grief process.

After my daughter's death, we met with an experienced pastor and his wife who had lost a teenage son through tragic circumstances several years earlier. *My friends, Tony and Susan, suggested that I limit my counseling time with students.* "Hurt people will hurt people" is the phrase that they shared with me as they explained what had happened in their own lives and ministry.

When someone comes to a leader for pastoral care, the person is focused completely on his or her own personal needs and problems. If the counselor is suffering, the personal pain in his or her own heart will fail to register a blip on the awareness screen of the other person. Many times the counselee's personal problems will seem small in comparison with the loss the counselor is battling in his or her own life. At this point it is easy to communicate through the filter of a harsh attitude that projects the following: "Are you kidding? Go get a real problem and then come back and see me. You don't even know what pain is."

We would never say those words, of course, but our heart attitudes will always communicate more *deeply* than actual words. Recognizing the truth that my friends were sharing, I reluctantly accepted their counsel. I am now so thankful that I heeded their wise words for a *season*, so the healing process could begin in my own life.

*To hide inside of protective walls for an extended duration of time, however, negates the possibility of complete healing and fruitfulness.* God has created us in His image, which means in part that we are created for community. Consequently, when we cut ourselves off from others, we create a stagnant environment that alienates us from *both* comfort and healing.

Healing is more than having an experience that gives something to me alone. Healing and fruitfulness are experienced most fully when we give to *others* out of our pain. I want to show this principle in the life of Joseph, and then illustrate it personally through my own walk of grief.

## JOSEPH'S EXAMPLE

The story of Joseph begins with the prophetic dreams given to him by God. Perhaps we could fault Joseph for lacking wisdom in the *way* that he shared these revelations with his family. His brothers were jealous of him, so maybe he should have kept silent for a time, but *nothing* in the recorded conduct of Joseph should have ever produced the type of treatment received from his closest family.

The Scripture can be brutally honest, and we read that his brothers "hated him and could not speak a kind word to him" (Genesis 37:4). In subsequent verses, we find that they "hated him all the more," and he also experienced harsh rebukes from his father (8, 10).

As we begin to follow his story, think about living in a home environment so charged with hatred and jealousy that not *one* kind word is spoken. This is the daily experience of Joseph, a sensitive young man of 17, who loves God with all his heart. How does Joseph respond in this painful family turmoil? Let's join him in his personal journey and see how God brings him to healing and fruitfulness, gracing him to give and to forgive as he serves others.

His brothers have migrated to Shechem for the purpose of grazing their sheep, and Jacob is concerned about their welfare. He calls his favored son, Joseph, to his side and asks him to visit his brothers to ascertain any needs they might have.

Basically, Joseph is being asked to go on a pastoral journey and minister care to people who hate him with every fiber of their being. Joseph could respond in any number of different ways.

One response could be to say, "No way! My brothers hate me. I'll only receive more abuse if I go. Let them work out their own problems, or let someone else make the trip."

Instead, Joseph responds with humility and obedience as he leaves the valley of Hebron to express practical love to brothers who despise him. He makes a choice to give to others out of his pain.

The continuation of the story is horrendous. His brothers see him coming from a distance and, fueled by their hatred, decide to kill him (Genesis 37:18). In their original murderous plot, they don't even plan to bury him. They figure they'll just "throw him into one of these cisterns" and walk away (19).

It's only the intercession of Reuben and Judah that saves Joseph's life as they adopt an alternative plan to make some extra money and sell their *brother* into slavery. *We are witnessing the family of God functioning at its dysfunctional worst!*

Only God knows the anguish that is in Joseph's spirit as he travels in chains with the Ishmaelites to Egypt. After his arrival, he is sold again, and his pain intensifies. In Egypt, however, the suffering of Joseph is qualified by one important phrase that makes *all* the difference in anyone's life. "The Lord was with Joseph and he prospered" (39:2). If we know God is with us, it's possible to walk through the most awful circumstances with the reassurance that our lives are in His hands.

*"If we know God is with us, it's possible to walk through the most awful circumstances with the reassurance that our lives are in His hands."*

Interestingly, Joseph finds himself serving a master with a certain measure of spiritual insight. Potiphar sees "that the Lord was with him," and so he entrusts Joseph with the care of everything he has.

After a time, Potiphar's wife notices Joseph's good looks and powerful build and attempts to seduce him day after day (6-7). This is no accident. It is a scheme of the enemy. Whenever we find ourselves in the throes of personal suffering, the enemy will attack us with many temptations because pain makes us *vulnerable*. It would be easy for Joseph to rationalize his temptation with distorted thinking: "Nothing is going right for me, and I deserve this sexual diversion. Why should I serve God anyway after all that's happened to me?"

Instead, Joseph refuses to yield and receive the *momentary* and *counterfeit* comfort that an illicit affair could provide. He will do nothing that damages his relationship with God.

Potiphar's wife responds to Joseph's rejection with lies and slander, telling her husband that his trusted servant has tried to rape her. His Egyptian master responds to this malicious lie with harsh anger and has Joseph thrown into prison.

How is it possible for these things to happen in the life of a man who loves God so completely? Surely now Joseph will become bitter and stop serving God *and* others, won't he?

He is doing *everything* right and finds himself slipping into even deeper suffering and pain. Looking back through the scriptural record, we are confronted again with the incredible phrase that defines Joseph's prison experience: "While Joseph was there in the prison, the Lord was with him" (Genesis 39:21). God granted Joseph favor in the eyes of the prison warden, and we read the beautiful footnote that the Lord "showed him kindness."

We are reminded here of an observation that we made in our last chapter. It might not *feel* as though God is with me, and with the natural eye it's difficult to see His *kindness*. Joseph could well have thought— *If this is kindness, please never show me meanness or harshness.*

Faith and trust, however, will refuse to look only at the external surface of things. As we like to remind ourselves in worship services, God is good *all* the time! In the most distressing circumstances, Joseph is confident of God's presence and kindness.

Joseph could have isolated himself in anger and frustration in the midst of his newest downturn—but he chooses instead to sacrificially give to the Lord *and* others by faithfully serving the warden and *seeking* out ways to minister to the other prisoners.

After he interprets the dreams of the cupbearer and baker, his heart is filled with hope for a release from prison. The cupbearer promises Joseph, if he is restored to his place of influence, that he will do everything in his power to secure Joseph's freedom. The words that Joseph speaks to Pharaoh's servant at this point are revealing: "'I have done nothing to deserve being put in a dungeon'" (Genesis 40:15). Joseph recognizes that his suffering is *not* related to personal rebellion and sin. He knows that God has been with him and seems confident that this will be the hour of his deliverance. Sadly, when the cupbearer is fully restored, he completely *forgets* about Joseph.

We see here the clear experiential progression of Psalm 42 as was previously discussed. In his early dreams, the *deep* in God was calling to the *deep* in Joseph: "Do you want to minister to your brothers and save your entire family?"

Joseph responded with a wholehearted *yes* and was ready to lay hold of his eternal destiny—but now the spiritual waves and breakers have washed over his life. He is experiencing complete brokenness, produced by *undeserved* pain and suffering in his life. Every test that he successfully passes, qualifies him for a more severe trial.

*"Joseph has made a choice in each of these circumstances not only to love God, but also to serve others in the experience of personal pain."*

Abuse, a pit, slavery and prison have been his reward for unswerving faithfulness and devotion to the Lord.

Joseph has made a choice in each of these circumstances not only to love God, but also to serve others in the experience of personal pain. In the midst of suffering, he has continued to give to others. The *seeds* of love and obedience that Joseph has planted in his thirteen years of intensifying losses are now about to produce a *harvest* of healing and fruitfulness.

Joseph is brought out of prison to serve the entire nation of Egypt, even receiving the signet ring of Pharaoh. He is blessed with a wife and two sons. He names his firstborn Manasseh (*forget*) because God had caused him "to forget all his trouble." His second son is named Ephraim (*twice fruitful*) to indicate how "fruitful" God had made him in "the land of his suffering" (Genesis 41:52-53).

His ultimate fruitfulness is demonstrated by the fulfillment of God's Word in his life. From his place of power and influence, he is now able to save his entire family from starvation, even extending *kindness* to the ones who hurt him most deeply. "'You intended to harm me,'" he declares, "'but God intended it for good to accomplish what is now being done, the saving of many lives'" (50:20).

Note how our current principle is fulfilled in the life of this great leader. In the early stages of pain, he *gives* to his brothers. As a slave in Egypt, he *gives* his service to a master. In the deepest levels of suffering, he *serves* a whole prison, ministering perhaps to thousands of prisoners. Now in his exaltation, he *serves* an entire nation, positioning himself simultaneously to *save* his family from extinction.

Clearly, Joseph has experienced *both* healing and fruitfulness. The names of his children give daily testimony to the reality of being able to forget the horror of his pain. He also illustrates that it's possible to walk through horrible things and still have a spirit preserved from bitterness. For these things to happen, however, it's necessary to make a dual choice.

*In our deepest anguish, we must not only choose to surrender ourselves to God, but also choose to give to others out of our pain.* These choices *release* the full power of Christ's healing and fruitfulness in our own lives.

## PERSONAL ILLUSTRATION

After the death of my daughter and granddaughter, I felt like a wounded animal and wanted to crawl into a corner and die. In my daily interaction with others, I dreaded the normal conversational questions of "How are you doing?" or "What's up?"

"You really don't want to know what's up" is how I would have liked to respond. Being in full-time ministry made these interactions more difficult. Prolonged seclusion was impossible because my whole life and vocation were defined by serving God and others.

I fondly remembered a factory job I had worked years earlier, where I had stood for nine hours a day grinding out electric insulators on a lathe. My social interactions had been limited on that job, and I longed for the experience of those days again.

Let me just note here that *grief is a powerful thief*. It *steals* enthusiasm, desire and passion as it drains our zest for life. It surely had stolen all of mine, and I found myself attempting to hide in my home at night, watching hours of television in an attempt to escape the excruciating agony of my life through mindless diversion. I didn't want to talk, preach, teach, exercise, read, study or listen to music. When possible, I sought complete isolation from others in my pain.

One of the first personal ministry decisions I faced was whether to teach my *Marriage and Family* class. At the time of my daughter's death, this was a class I had taught for 18 years. Most of the life principles I sought to impart in my class were drawn from my family relationships. Coupled with the lessons learned from counseling and pastoral ministry, stories from life with my wife and children were the source of countless illustrations, providing the foundation upon which the content of my course rested.

As I began to prepare my heart for teaching this yearly class, I realized how deeply my daughter, René, was woven into the very fabric of my teaching. The challenge of teaching this course in the upcoming fall semester seemed overwhelming, and I seriously considered stepping back from my responsibility and letting someone else do it. Backing away from something I felt God had called me to do seemed impossible, however, so with deep apprehension and uncertainty I launched into the class five months later.

In many respects, the experience of those 16 weeks was like swimming through a sea of peanut butter. Each class was taught through a haze of emotional pain. I felt like dropping to my knees and crying out in agony every time I used my children as an illustration. At times, I felt as though I would be unable to continue because the memories of my departed daughter were so precious and fragrant in my heart and mind. *I was able to persevere only by embracing daily the grace of God.* It was impossible for me to imagine how my life would look in future months or years. I survived only with the trust that His grace would help me through *that* day.

The response of my students during these weeks still amazes me to the present day. I would never have believed that it was possible for *anyone* to receive positive impartation from a person so emotionally crippled. All of my teaching was being filtered through the grid of a broken heart.

With few exceptions, however, the students who sat under my ministry that semester approached me with overwhelming affirmation. What I received was much *more* than simple encouragement along the lines of "not bad, considering what a terrible mess you are." So many, instead, shared gratitude for the deep impartation of life that had been deposited in their spirits. "You will never know how you have blessed my life" was a statement that I heard over and over again.

*"If we choose to give to others out of our anguish, not only will we encounter personal healing and fruitfulness, but also our lives will become a blessing to others in need."*

A pattern began to emerge through the fog of my pain. If we choose to give to others out of our anguish, not only will we encounter personal healing and fruitfulness, but also our lives will become a blessing to others in need.

This pattern was forever established in the foundation of my life through another series of ministry experiences. In 1999, I received an invitation to minister in the war-torn country of Bosnia-Herzegovina. This invitation came three years after the death of my girls and four years after the ending of the horrendous Bosnian civil war.

I struggled over accepting the invitation because of my ongoing experience of daily pain. The invitation package included a week of intensive ministry in the newly-founded Mostar Bible School, as well as speaking engagements in other key cities of Bosnia-Herzegovina. There was also the possibility of ministry in the neighboring country of Croatia.

I questioned my ability to do it. The ministry responsibilities in my own designated sphere seemed to be all that I could handle. In these areas, I had developed a certain *comfortable* rhythm that allowed me to function successfully, but accepting the demands of a major overseas trip seemed overwhelming.

After two days of pondering the decision in my own heart, I had decided to decline when the gentle nudge of the Holy Spirit reminded me that I hadn't included my Lord in the decision.

"Okay, Jesus," I prayed with confident assurance, "surely You don't expect me to go." Sometimes, the Lord can be so unreasonable! I was shocked when He prompted me to walk through His "open door."

Being keenly aware that the doors "He opens no one can shut" (Revelation 3:7), I began to protest. My protesting eventually evolved into pleading. "This doesn't even seem wise," I said in agitated exasperation. Realizing that I couldn't talk God out of His "unwise" decision was coupled with a lack of desire to be a modern-day Jonah. Not really wanting to be swallowed by a very large "fish of circumstances," I finally said *yes*.

The trip was going to be quite expensive, which meant I had to trust God for extra finances.

"Maybe the money that I need won't be provided," I reasoned, "and I can still get my own way." Not so!

Without any requests or letters being sent out, the money actually came to me in a matter of weeks, with a *surplus* to take as blessings for the churches where I would be ministering.

"Okay, God," I said, still a little aggravated, "I get it! To Bosnia I will go."

*It's extremely difficult to put into words the depth of what God did in my heart during my first visit (there would be two more) to this incredible Eastern European country.* My first impressions were focused on the awful devastation that had been done to the physical structure of the nation. Even though the war had been over for four years, there was still not one area of city *or* countryside that did not bear the scars of an evil civil war.

When I first arrived in 1999, there were still *millions* of unexploded landmines in the country. It was emotionally stirring to watch U.N. peacekeeping forces working in the fields and public areas of cities, slowly attempting to "de-mine" vast tracks of land.

Two weeks before I arrived, a mine had killed a seven-year-old girl as she was playing behind her own home. It seemed awful beyond words that a precious little girl was not safe playing in her own backyard.

The bombed-out buildings and wounded land, however, were only the tip of the iceberg. The real heartbreaking story was found in the faces of the amazing people who lived there. *How do you calculate the toll of pain and suffering in a country that has been shredded by war?*

I forced myself to visit three large cemeteries in one of Bosnia's largest cities. I wept as I walked along and looked at thousands of new graves and markers, mostly for young men who had lost the gift of life while in their twenties. I shook my head in shock as I realized the country had lost nearly an entire generation of young men.

The emotional assault on my senses was almost more than I could bear. At some points, I felt like screaming at the outrage of such senseless loss.

During my first ministry time in Bosnia-Herzegovina, I never met a single family that had not lost someone in the war. One sister in the Bible school had lost *all* three of her sons in the murderous carnage.

The wounds that I had observed on the land were nothing compared to the pain etched into the faces, eyes and souls of the gracious people I met there. Under the cover of a humanitarian organization, I was allowed to enter and minister in two of the many refugee camps. The poverty was unspeakable, and the accommodations and facilities inadequate. People were forced to sleep in shifts inside temporary shelters able to hold only 20 people at a time. Lost homes, lost occupations, lost families and lost lives! It was a country inundated with pain, grief and loss.

One of the first things that struck my heart like a hammer blow was how everyone accepted these losses as a normal part of life. People were not complaining and asking, "How could this happen to me?" There were no *special* cases because suffering and loss had hurt every family.

This understanding is very different from our North American perspective. After our girls' funeral, we received hundreds of cards and letters from friends and people who had been touched by our ministry. We often received comments that went something like this: "What happened to you is one of the worst things I ever heard. I don't know if I would be able to survive the loss of one of my children."

The implication of that statement is that our family had been singled out for something highly *unusual*, that something like this happens only in *rare* cases and is the exception to the rule.

One person offered a particularly painful assessment: "You are an example to us all," my friend declared, "and I find comfort in the feeling that, because it happened to you, it won't happen to me." I didn't know how to respond. The person might just as well have said, "I was close when lightning struck *you*, so I believe the averages are now in my favor that it won't happen to *me*. Your terrible loss means that my family will be okay." I knew of no other way to interpret the "comfort" that was being offered to me.

It was impossible to have such thoughts as I stood in Bosnia-Herzegovina. My suffering and pain were *not* the most awful thing that these people had ever seen. In fact, most had suffered more severely. Comparing sufferings on a graded scale is never productive or healthy, but my heart was sensitized as I realized I now belonged to a fraternity that was larger than I had ever imagined.

As I ministered in different geographical settings, I shared my personal testimony of loss for the purpose of illustration in my teaching and preaching. The long-term missionaries told me they were observing a great openness of heart in the people as they responded to my ministry. In their assessment, this openness was deeper than what had been extended to other ministering guests. I didn't fully understand what they were seeing until I experienced a moment in the city of Sarajevo that will be etched on my heart forever.

*"Comparing sufferings on a graded scale is never productive or healthy, but my heart was sensitized as I realized I now belonged to a fraternity that was larger than I had ever imagined."*

On that particular day, I had the blessing of ministering in a newly-birthed church of about 100 people. The church was experiencing growth and had only that week poured a concrete foundation for a new building. There had recently been violent threats made towards the church, so the congregation hearing my preaching was accompanied by armed U.N. forces from the country of France. It was my first experience of preaching with machine gun "accessories" in the first row, but the show of force gave the illusion of safety. I preached from the gospel of John, and I illustrated my message with a testimony related to my daughter's death.

After the service, the pastor and a lady who had attended that morning gave me a tour of the city. As we traveled through Sarajevo, the woman abruptly pointed to one of the bombed-out buildings. "That was my apartment building during the war!" she exclaimed.

As I stared at the rubble, the pastor stopped the car while she shared her story in more detail.

"The shelling had been going on for hours," she said, "but suddenly it stopped." During these brief reprieves, she explained, people would cautiously venture out from their homes to buy bread and fresh water on the black market.

"My husband and I had three daughters," she continued, "and we decided to let my husband stay with them because they were so terrified." She herself went out, was successful in purchasing the basic supplies and was moving towards her home when the shelling started again.

As she arrived at her building, she discovered that her apartment had taken a direct hit. The horrific conclusion of her story involved walking into the rubble of her living room to discover her husband and three daughters dead on the floor.

"I never got a chance to say good-bye," she said softly.

There was a moment of complete silence in the automobile as my emotional circuits blew fuses. I heard the silence break at the sound of my own sobbing. In my brokenness and tears, I gently touched her hand and said, "I am so sorry . . . I cannot understand that kind of senseless loss."

I will never forget her response as she looked back into my eyes, "Oh, but you can understand," she said, "because it makes no sense that your daughter died eating a piece of fish."

I will always cherish that moment as one of the most sacred ministry times of my life. I reflected for days on what my sister-in-Christ had said to me, and a powerful truth began to work a new measure of healing into my soul. *Not only was I being healed because I was giving to others out of my pain, but my experience of loss had assisted me in making a life connection with another person that would have been otherwise impossible.* I am *not* suggesting God took my girls so I could exercise more effective ministry, but He used the experience of my pain to touch the life of another hurting person. For the first time since the funeral, I began to feel a measure of validation and understanding in my loss.

The reality of this principle has been demonstrated over and over again in my ministry, not only in three trips to that country, but in all spheres of influence to which I have been called. *People who have suffered deeply immediately recognize the presence of that experience in the life of another person.* This recognition in turn produces an openness of heart that facilitates the possibility of deeply imparting truth from life to life.

When we choose to give to others out of our pain, we experience deeper healing, fruitfulness *and* increased effectiveness in touching the lives of others. As I pondered this truth in my heart, I formulated the following question: *How* does this happen? As we turn again to the pages of Scripture, we find *one* answer expressed in *three* parts.

## THE ANSWER

The *first* part of the answer is that we are brought into deeper relationship with the "Father of compassion and the God of all comfort" (2 Corinthians 1:3). This reality has become very precious to me.

When we come to God, we enter into relationship with the One who is infinite. There are *no* limitations in God. This is the foundation of our justification as stated in Romans 5. Paul tells us clearly "where sin increased, grace increased all the more" (20). As a finite human being, my entire existence is marked by limitations. This applies even to my sin because there is a limit to how bad I can be— even in the expression of my deepest depravity. God, however, knows no such limitations in the extension of His grace. The depths of my sin can never nullify His grace that brings "eternal life through Jesus Christ our Lord." *My finite sin is swallowed up by His infinite grace.*

This same principle applies to God's compassionate comfort. Paul stresses that He is able to comfort "us in *all* our troubles," which would be a ridiculous claim if our Lord were anything less than infinite. The comfort that we can extend from heart to heart will never be able to touch all the areas of another's personal pain. The God who sees it all is able to bring comfort into the deepest recesses of every single hurt. Because He is infinite, this comfort is not limited— even when encountering my most horrendous pain. My deepest hurt is not capable of draining the inexhaustible well of comfort that He makes available to those who turn to Him.

After our girls died, I was *inundated* by grief, pain and loss. I have shared in an earlier chapter how God impressed Matthew 5:4 on our hearts: "'Blessed are those who mourn, for they shall be comforted.'" If we embrace the mourning process, this becomes God's *promise* to us. The words of Jesus are clear: It's not that we might, but that we will be comforted. The promise is sure.

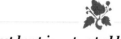

*"My deepest hurt is not capable of draining the inexhaustible well of comfort that He makes available to those who turn to Him."*

Paul's summary to the church at Corinth is this: "Just as the *sufferings* of Christ flow over into our lives, so also through Christ our *comfort* overflows" (2 Corinthians 1:5, emphasis added). The river of our pain is no match for the ocean of His comfort.

The *second* truth contained in this passage of Scripture is that we are *enabled* to *impart* comfort into the lives of others. Having testified that "through Christ our comfort overflows," Paul assures the Corinthians—"if we are distressed, it is for your salvation and comfort" (6).

My ministry trips to a war-ravaged country taught me that existential pain and suffering are *universal*. My shattering losses didn't constitute something unusual or even extraordinary. People are hurting in every area of the globe, and they are crying out for comfort. Who will be able to fill this gap and meet the need? The answer is staggering and profound in its simplicity: *We give away to others the comfort we have received from God.*

We must never forget that we are only *channels* of comfort. Left to myself, I have nothing to give to anyone. Without Christ, I fear I might have taken my life in response to the pain that washed over me daily. But Jesus promised a Comforter to all who would receive Him. I don't have to go to a remote geographical location to receive this comfort—it's imparted by the Person of the Holy Spirit who dwells within me.

The comfort that the Holy Spirit brings to us must flow through us and touch other hurting people. If we receive and don't give, we spiritually implode and can even sink deeper into a pit of despair. As we give away the comfort that we have received, *we* experience deeper healing. This explains the force of Paul's words when he declares that "if we are comforted, it is for your comfort, which produces in you patient endurance of the same sufferings we suffer" (2 Corinthians 1:6).

The *third* part of our answer is rooted in the truth that suffering brings us into *deeper dependence* on God. As Paul continues his exposition on suffering, he makes a personal application to his own life and ministry. We don't "want you to be uninformed" about the "hardships we suffered," he declares openly. His words become even more focused as he describes the experience of being under "great pressure" far beyond his "ability to endure." The graphic conclusion of his testimony is given with this intense description: "We despaired even of life," and in "our hearts felt the sentence of death" (8-9).

Paul is proclaiming the reality of his intense suffering *without* exaggeration. He had despaired of life itself as he felt the claws of death enclose his heart. In encountering this kind of pain, he offers a simple explanation and application. This happened so that we would "not rely on ourselves, but on God who raises the dead."

When life is running smoothly, it's incredibly easy to coast spiritually as we rely on our own wisdom, strength and resources. Of course, we are *always* in great need of God, even in situations where the gravity of our need is not clearly perceived. But when all of the wheels fall off and we find ourselves despairing of life, the necessity of complete dependency inescapably washes over us in powerful waves. Paul is stating this truth as bluntly as possible: *Without Christ, he would have died in the experience of pain and suffering.*

We can understand this testimony in the experience of our own devastating personal losses. When a loved one dies, we lose our marriage, our health fails, or we lose our job and retirement package, we are faced with death itself. Our need becomes desperate with the growing awareness that, *without* Him, we will not make it.

But this passage in 2 Corinthians gives us a wonderful redeeming insight. Our desperation in pain and loss drives us into deeper *dependency* on the "God of all comfort." In circumstances that confront us with death, we encounter the One who "raises the dead." The same power that brought Jesus forth from the grave is made available to me in my personal pain. He is able to redeem my greatest losses *because* of His infinite comfort and resurrection life. These three principles given by Paul provide the New Testament foundation for the experience of healing and fruitfulness as we *give to others out of our pain.*

## SUMMARY

**The natural response in the experience of grief and loss is to retreat into our own personal world and build walls of protection.** Left to ourselves, we pull the blanket of despair over our heads and crawl into the corner to die. Although a certain measure of healing can be experienced in solitude, the deepest redemption and fruitfulness will be produced only as we *choose* to give to others in the experience of our pain.

**In this process, we are drawn into deeper relationship with God as we discover the fulfillment that comes in touching the lives of other hurting people.** We also encounter in a most powerful way the resurrection life of Christ Himself as He miraculously produces life from our experience of death, pain and loss. Serving other hurting people almost completes the healing cycle, as we experience true transformation and fruitfulness. The principle of the next chapter, however, takes us one step further as God closes the healing loop in our lives.

# CHAPTER 7

# The Miracle

### Principle 6:
### *Healing and fruitfulness are experienced when we open our hearts to receive new blessing.*

W e come now to the consideration of our last principle. The thoughts expressed in this chapter not only close the circle of the healing process, but also point us to a great miracle that can occur in the grief walk: the experience of fruitfulness in the form of *new* blessing.

One of the common longings we experience in the early days of any loss is the hope that our lives will return to *normal*. How often I have heard the statement made by someone in the throes of debilitating pain—"I can't wait until my life returns to normal."

*We must be absolutely clear about this intense desire: Things will never be normal again.* Our lives can never be as they were before, and we'll never experience or reclaim life the way it *used to be*.

The painful reality of serious loss requires the embracing of this truth if we hope to experience healing and fruitfulness. If we have lost our marriage, health or loved one, we must say *good-bye* forever to the "normal" that defined our past. A child, for example, who experiences sexual abuse can never again return to innocence because the horrible violation has stolen it forever. Understanding this harsh reality is what makes the losses of life so intensely painful.

After our daughter's death, we were forced into confrontation with the devastating truth that the old normal was gone forever. In many ways, it seemed as though a huge eraser had blotted out our future. My daughter had been on the launching pad of her life, but death meant I would never be able to see it unfold. I know that she would have been an incredible mother, but the big eraser of loss permanently wiped out the experience of seeing her lead and nurture her own family.

Furthermore, we were confronted with the fact that we would never share another Christmas or birthday together. The joy of hearing her voice on the telephone, or embracing her as I kissed her beautiful blonde hair, all these and other things beyond counting were gone forever, taken away by circumstances that crashed into our lives out of nowhere. My past *and* future were altered irrevocably as old norms were swept away into the abyss.

Refusing to accept the loss of the old normal is unhealthy because it plants our lives in the spiritual quicksand of denial. Denial can be expressed in different ways. One possibility is trying to preserve the old pattern in the absence of what has been lost. Sometimes, this results in creating a kind of shrine, where a child's room is left untouched and preserved *exactly* the way it was when she died. Every object and poster must remain in place, as if the loved one might someday return to her room.

Sometimes, people act out denial by escaping through self-destructive behavior, even returning to addictions that have overpowered them in the past. The overwhelming *power* of personal pain *can* drive us to find counterfeit relief, even traveling roads we already know lead nowhere.

Moving in these unhealthy patterns of denial produces bitter fruit that makes us sick in our souls. Not only does our hurt remain *unhealed*, but we face the added pain of "solutions" that provide no answers. When denial is coupled with the inevitable consequences of self-destructive behavior, a person is pushed into even deeper despair. In certain extreme cases, this can produce attempted or actual suicide.

If the old normal is lost, we must ask for God's help in developing the reality of a new normal, which is defined in two ways. Firstly, we must learn a new way of walking that compensates for the loss, seeing that loss can be defined as a dramatic taking away or amputation. In many ways, it's like the loss of a limb or the loss of one of the five senses.

Take, for example, a person who has lost his eyesight. Not being able to see doesn't negate personhood, *nor* the ability to function in life. It does, however, bring permanent change to a person's life: Things will *never* be the way they were before, and a new normal must be discovered and defined.

This was powerfully illustrated to me during an afternoon spent with a blind pianist. My friend had lost his sight in childhood but had persevered in his piano studies. His artistic ability was nothing short of genius, and he could play anything from jazz to classical to rock and roll.

One of the compensations for this brother was the ability to hear things that I totally missed. I received a personal blessing in the course of one afternoon when we sat together and he taught me how to "hear" a piece of music. I love and listen to a lot of music as part of my regular lifestyle, but I have never listened to any music recording the same since that afternoon. Because of the learned compensations produced by his new normal, he taught me something I would have missed on my own.

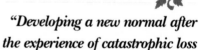

*"Developing a new normal after the experience of catastrophic loss can equip us with something new with which to bless others."*

This is the way of healing in spiritual losses as well. Developing a new normal after the experience of catastrophic loss can equip us with something new with which to bless others. Finding and defining this new normal is different for each person and can be discovered only by confronting the reality of loss and receiving over time the restorative miracles that Jesus will add to our lives.

The second part of defining the new normal deals with heart attitudes and a decision of our will. Will we be *open* to embrace the new blessing when God sends it? Thinking about this reality is intense because we can choose to accept *or* reject the new gift that Jesus brings.

If we surrender to the healing process after losing something precious, I believe that it's possible to experience new grace. This new blessing is not a *substitute* for what has been lost but a *gift* that could never have been given if the loss had not occurred. Everything within us screams that this is impossible. How can *anything* positive arise from the ashes of grief? We turn now to one classic example from Scripture to answer that question.

## GOD'S RESTORATION IN THE BOOK OF HAGGAI

The book of Haggai reveals the principles of God's restoration in the aftermath of catastrophic loss. The Jews have returned to the Promised Land to rebuild their temple. Seventy years before, the nation of Babylonia had conquered Judah and taken God's people into slavery. The city of Jerusalem had been devastated and burned, turning the beautiful temple that Solomon had built into a pile of rubble.

To better understand the significance of the prophecy that Haggai will give, it's important to consider a piece of earlier history related to the building and dedication of Solomon's temple. King David had deeply desired the privilege of building a temple to honor the Lord. When it was prophetically revealed he was not the chosen leader to perform this task, he had made plans and provisions for his son, Solomon, to accomplish its construction. When Solomon had completed the project, he planned an elaborate dedication service, culminating in a prayer he offered while kneeling on an elevated bronze platform.

Just before Solomon prayed, the priests, Levites, musicians and singers were all giving praise and thanks to the Lord, crying in unison, "'He is good; His love endures forever'" (2 Chronicles 5:11-13). God responded to this worship by filling the temple with His presence in such an intense way, that the "priests could not perform their service" because of the glory cloud that filled the temple (2 Chronicles 5:14).

Solomon then prayed a powerfully anointed prayer, asking that *all* the peoples of the earth would be able to know the Lord personally as His people Israel did (6:33). As Solomon concludes this prayer, God responds again.

We are told that "fire came down from heaven" and the glory of the Lord filled the temple once more. For a second time, the priests could not enter the temple because of God's intense presence. All the people could do was kneel "on the pavement with their faces to the ground" as they continued to give thankful worship to God (7:1-3).

On the site where that incredible event occurred, Haggai's generation presently stands. There is no glory cloud now—only devastated piles of rubble that have been partially cleared to lay the foundation for a new temple. It's in this context the prophet now appears on the scene to give encouragement and hope.

At first, his words don't seem to be very encouraging because he asks three questions that actually seem cruel: "'"Who of you is left who saw this house in its former glory? How does it look to you now? Does it seem to you like nothing?"'" (Haggai 2:3).

"Thanks for nothing!" might have been the natural response of the people to these questions. "Are you kidding, Haggai, or are you just mean and sarcastic? Of course, it seems like nothing. We're standing here with only a foundation and piles of rubble. You're asking us to compare *that* with the glorious outpouring of God's presence under Solomon? Why don't you go and encourage someone else?"

But Haggai isn't finished. He challenges the religious/political leaders and *all* of the people with these words: "'"Be strong, and work . . . for I am with you," declares the Lord Almighty'" (4).

He continues by making several remarkable statements. He first asserts that God promises to shake the heavens and earth, the sea and dry land and all the nations of the earth. This shaking will produce the building of a new temple.

Secondly, God promises not only that this new temple will be filled with His glory, """but that the glory of this present house will be greater than the glory of the former house""" (Haggai 2:9).

This reveals the miraculous nature of God's healing and restoration. *He not only restores but brings something new that could never have been experienced if the old normal were still in place.*

From the perspective of Scripture, Haggai's prophecy is fulfilled in Hebrews 12:25-29 where Haggai 2:6 is quoted. The greater glory is fulfilled in the Church of the Firstborn, a new temple, made of people that will not lodge only in one city, but literally fill the whole earth with God's glory (Hebrews 12:22-23). This, of course, is God's *answer* to what Solomon had prayed for hundreds of years earlier.

Just as He came to His temple with a promise and purpose to bring a "greater glory," the presence of the Lord comes into the lives of individual people in the midst of devastation, pain and hopelessness—people who are part of the "new temple" that will show forth His glory in the earth. "I am with you" is the promise He *always* brings to our crisis and hurt. This promise is vital because loss produces the shaking of life's very foundations. Without the Lord's help, a person can potentially wander without purpose for years, caught in the strangling bondage of unhealed pain. But Haggai reveals this important principle of God's Kingdom: *Divine shakings bring new resources that produce a new blessing that can never be imagined.*

I believe this principle applies powerfully in the area of grief and loss. It has certainly been proven in my life. The death of my daughter and granddaughter left me emotionally in a pile of devastated rubble, and I wasn't sure that I would ever feel joy again. It was difficult to embrace *any* hope for my future, let alone a vision for healing and fruitfulness that would produce overflowing joy in my life again. But that is exactly what God *can* do, and what He *did* do for me. It's from the foundation of this *new* joy and blessing that I now share the miracle of restoration that God brought to our family.

### OUR MIRACLE

The pain of any loss must be shared within the network of relationships we have with family and friends. This means that we not only hurt at a personal level, but also must monitor what the loss is doing to those we love. The people in our lives still need us, and this produces frustration because of the enforced limitations brought by a broken heart.

*"The pain of any loss must be shared within the network of relationships we have with family and friends."*

My elderly parents (now with the Lord) serve as one example of this difficult reality. In 1946, 50 years before René's death, my parents had buried a son (my older brother) who had died in a tragic drowning accident before I was born. My father had never dealt with this horrendous loss by walking through the redemptive *process* of grief and mourning.

After the death of his beloved granddaughter, my dad was forced to revisit this unhealed pain in his own life and, as a consequence, found it difficult to cope with the new loss. The resulting tension that this unresolved pain created in his life contributed in part to his own death three years later. It broke my heart to see my parents torn in this new struggle, but my own pain handicapped me in my ability to help.

Our beloved daughter, Danielle, was also an integral part of the inner circle of our pain. She had been "joined-at-the-hip" best friends with her older sister, and after losing René, she refused for a season to walk in paths of healing—choosing self-destructive denial instead.

My wife and I will be eternally grateful for how our daughter over time began to make healthy choices and returned to the Lord and the inner circle of her family. The depth of love and friendship that we now share with our younger daughter produces thankfulness in our hearts every day. In the early days of our grief, however, we felt crushed as we watched what was happening to our priceless living treasure in the choices she was making.

Also involved in the personal network of mourning was our beloved son-in-law. There are certain things that must be said about this incredible man. First and foremost, we will always be thankful for how he honored the memory and life of our daughter in the way that he grieved for her. He was always a "straight arrow" as he moved toward the target of genuine healing and fruitfulness.

Because of his character, gifts *and* looks, there were a number of young women who sought relationship with Doug in the aftermath of René's death. Our son-in-law would allow no deviations because he understood that there were no shortcuts in this process of grief and mourning. Whole and healthy people make healthy relationships, and Doug knew he would have nothing to give in a new relationship until he experienced substantial healing.

Even before Doug had courted our daughter, we had developed a close relationship with him. We deeply loved him before he loved our daughter. In the aftershocks of collective loss, we all committed to maintain this closeness for the rest of our lives. For many months, we talked several times a week on the phone and were together as much as 550 miles of geographical separation would allow, spending Thanksgiving, Christmas and summer vacations together, often with his parents, who were our friends and were also in mourning themselves.

Doug and René had purchased and moved into a beautiful new home about six months before she died. It was a spacious four-bedroom home they planned to fill with children. Their new home was strategically located close to their church because they loved the church and wanted their children to grow into that same love. The house had been made ready for the arrival of their new daughter with special attention given to the nursery. Noah's ark was the theme, and all was in a state of readiness for the arrival of Jessica Grace.

Now the son of our hearts was rattling around in a huge empty house with no wife or daughter to make it the home of his dreams.

During our visits, we would grieve together and find a measure of comfort in one another's company—but whenever we left Doug to travel home, we would be overwhelmed with pain as we pulled out of the driveway. Our son was alone, and the whole scenario seemed so terribly wrong.

There were many deep, conflicting emotions that stirred within our hearts during this time. On one level, we were asking Jesus to bring another person into Doug's life. We all agreed that forming a new family needed to happen. *Somewhere* God had another young woman who would be so blessed by relationship with this wonderful man.

On the other hand, we struggled with a fair measure of anxiety—would there be a place for us in his new family? It seemed impossible that a new wife would have room in her heart for the family of the woman who had been married to her husband in the past. Would our cherished relationship with Doug end when this new woman appeared? We were trying hard to prepare our hearts for that daunting reality.

Coupled with our prayers for Doug was an understanding based on a foresight that God had given to my wife. Connie had shared with me early on in the grief process the belief that God would bring someone into Doug's life who would personally understand grief. Perhaps this understanding

*"Today, we can see that it was God's delight to answer our prayers and to allay our doubts and fears!"*

would help her to build a bridge with our family, but we had serious doubts on that point. Today, we can see that it was God's delight to answer our prayers and to allay our doubts and fears!

It was about four years after our loss that we encountered our *new* miracle. Our family had experienced genuine healing on many different levels because we had consistently done the hard work of grief and mourning. Healing *and* fruitfulness were beginning to manifest themselves in our lives. Our new beginning came with a call from Doug in the month of May and on the evening of Mother's Day. It started out like a normal Mother's Day call, with Doug expressing his love and appreciation for my wife. Then the conversation shifted into another gear.

"I've met someone," Doug said in a quiet voice, filled with joy and excitement.

Our hearts accelerated with mixed emotions. This was the announcement we had both prayed for *and* dreaded!

He began to share more details. "She went through a divorce right about the time René died. She has two incredible children—a six-year-old daughter, named Katherine, and a four-year-old son, named Daniel. We met as part of the worship team and have been slowly and cautiously building a relationship."

As the story continued to unfold, we began to have a witness in our hearts that God indeed was forming this new relationship. The joyous possibility of Doug's receiving the gift of a new family outweighed any possible pain we could potentially experience if he had to take steps back from us. We would never stand between him and a new beginning, so we fully entered into his excitement and expectant joy.

"Next month I am bringing Michelle and the children to meet you," he announced. *"I've told her that our relationship cannot proceed unless we have your blessing."*

After we hung up the phone, we felt overcome with emotion. We were humbled that Doug wanted to include us in this way, and yet apprehensive about having such a significant part to play.

The next few weeks were soaked in prayer and preparation as we looked forward to this appointed meeting. The anticipated day arrived, and it was early evening when I heard my wife say, "They just pulled in."

I raced to the back porch to see Doug's cobalt blue Pontiac Firebird pull into the parking space and watched the doors fly open. Michelle and her precious children walked across the asphalt, up the stairs into our kitchen and, most significantly, into our *hearts.*

From the first embrace, Michelle became our daughter and her children our grandchildren. It's difficult to put into words how profoundly this experience has impacted our *whole* family.

At the time of this writing, it has been nine years since that first meeting. Eight years of marriage for Doug and Michelle have added Anna and David, two more incredible and greatly beloved grandchildren. They have all become our family in the deepest and truest sense of the word. I would like to share one example that illustrates the deep father-daughter bond that has formed between Michelle and me.

About five years ago, I was updating our ministry bio to send to a pastor in connection with a marriage conference at which Connie and I would be speaking. I was adding the normal updates of personal facts—the number of years we had been married, the number of years in ministry and so forth. The family section of our bio at that time would have read something like this: "Stacy and Connie have two daughters and one granddaughter. Their older daughter and granddaughter are in the arms of Jesus."

As I was typing what had become the standard entry on my office computer, I felt emotionally overwhelmed with a powerful thought that stopped me in my word-processing tracks: *You don't have two daughters and one granddaughter; you have three daughters and five grandchildren. This really describes what I feel for Michelle and the children,* I thought, *but what would she feel if I wrote it that way?*

I picked up the phone and punched in her number for a mid-morning call. Michelle answered, and I tentatively articulated to her the question on my heart.

There was a moment of silence, and I thought perhaps I had violated an emotional boundary. But then I heard the sound of weeping as my girl's voice broke into sobs. "Oh, Dad," she said, "I *am* your daughter, and I would be so honored to be listed in your bio."

Suddenly, Michelle was not the only one crying. As we spoke affirmation and love to one another, I realized I was having a sacred conversation that would mark me forever. God had completed the cycle of healing and produced new fruit by bringing this incredible daughter into my life. As I hung up the phone, I continued to weep in a state of wonder because of the new blessing God had poured into our family.

At the risk of sounding redundant, I must strongly state again that Michelle, Katherine, Daniel, Anna and David were *not* substitutes for the loss of my René and Jessica. My daughter and granddaughter can *never* be replaced. People are not exchanged like bricks in a wall. My firstborn daughter was a priceless gift of God to my life, and she brought blessing and joy that can be described only as sublime. She was my first instructor in teaching me what it meant to truly call God my Father. My second-born, Danielle, would continue to teach me in that area to the present day. No person can *ever* be replaced after death and loss.

But God doesn't leave us in the rubble of our pain and grief. In the midst of shaken foundations, He promises His presence. He *is* with us and commits to help us in the rebuilding process. If our hearts are open, He desires to bring new grace and blessing that would never have come if the loss had not been experienced.

I don't fully understand *how* this works, but I know that Jesus doesn't play games with our lives. He's not a gambler playing some kind of high stakes poker in hopes that somehow we might become winners. Of course, there are many *why* questions that remain unanswered as we surrender to God in the painful experiences of life. Our King, however, is never out of control, and if I yield with a trusting heart, unspeakable new joy and blessing are restored to my life.

*"If our hearts are open, He desires to bring new grace and blessing that would never have come if the loss had not been experienced."*

At this juncture, it's of critical importance we recognize our part in the healing release of this truth principle. It's sobering to realize we have the power to *stop* the flow of any new blessing that God sends because we can choose to open *or* close our hearts to what He is giving us.

Our family could have chosen to remain in the rubble of grief and pain. We could have closed our hearts to the Lord and His three gifts that stepped out of a Pontiac Firebird on a warm June evening in 2000. It's *because* our hearts remained open that we were able to embrace the new people who rode into our lives, bringing deeper healing, increased fruitfulness and new blessing as they came.

If our wills are engaged to say *yes*, we can experience one of the great miracles of God's sovereignty—a restoration that releases His glory through our lives in a way that transcends *anything* we had formerly known.

It would be a great omission, however, to speak only of the grace and miracles that are released in our *present* lives. The amazing truth is that God has prepared an even greater miracle for our future, and to be silent about this hope is to miss the greatest *new* blessing of all.

## THE NEW BLESSING OF THE FUTURE

When we speak of this new blessing, called heaven, many people begin to shut down their spiritual receptors. "Don't talk to me about heaven" is a common attitude, and even in the Church there is a certain skepticism related to our eternal inheritance.

We have all heard these sarcastic expressions: "I don't care about a pie-in-the-sky,'" or, "That person is so heavenly minded that they are no earthly good." To focus on the blessings of a future heaven is deemed mystical, unscientific and irresponsible.

The biblical perspective is radically different. *God's promises for the future are what give meaning and substance to our present.* Paul states this truth with great forcefulness in his first letter to the church at Corinth: "If only for this life we have hope in Christ, we are to be pitied more than all men" (15:19).

It would be difficult to make a *more* extreme affirmation of our eternal future than what we read in that verse. I have heard some Christian people say that, even if there were no heaven, it would make no difference to them. Paul's response to these individuals is that he pities them. "You're pathetic" or "I feel really sorry for you" would be examples of contemporary paraphrases that would capture the essence of Paul's exhortation.

The focus of this chapter has been the new blessing that Christ brings to provide healing and fruitfulness in our experiences of pain and loss. Speaking of eternal inheritance does nothing to nullify anything we have said thus far because the certain hope of a *future* heaven is the foundation upon which our transient *present* is built.

The reason our foundation is so solid is that it's laid on the very *promise* of Christ: "'Do not let your hearts be troubled. Trust in God, trust also in Me. In My Father's house are many rooms; if it were not so I would have told you. I am going there to prepare a place for you. And if I go and prepare a place for you, I will come back, and take you to be with Me that you may also be where I am'" (John 14:1-3). The words of Jesus are instructive *and* comforting: God has created us for a Person and is preparing us for a place.

Accepting *both* of these spiritual realities is the only way to discover our spiritual true north as we find our way home. Paul clearly communicates that heaven *is* our home: "As long as we are at home in the body we are away from the Lord" (2 Corinthians 5:6). In the experience of death, we are "away from the body and at home with the Lord" (7-9).

Everything about our future hope is connected with *new* blessing. It's described by the apostle John as a "new heaven and a new earth" (Revelation 21:1). John's description focuses at first on our unbroken and perfect relationship with the King. We will be His people, and He will be our God (3). His vision continues by telling us what will be *missing* from our experience: "'There will be no more death, or mourning or crying or pain, for the old order of things has passed away'" (Revelation 21:4). The incredible conclusion to these promises comes from the mouth of the One who is seated on the throne as He declares with authority: "'I am making *everything* new!'" (5). As if that is not certainty enough, He commands that the vision should be written down, for "'these words are trustworthy and true'" (5).

All crying *related* to pain is *rooted* in loss. I may have lost my income, marriage, health or someone I've loved more than life itself. These losses bring pain, tears and even despair. Amid the rubble of our personal devastation, however, comes a divine shaking, producing new blessing for our present that could never have been anticipated. And this present blessing is only the beginning. The promises of Christ assure us of a *future* hope that everything will be made new as the great Chief Shepherd wipes away every tear from our eyes (4).

*"Amid the rubble of our personal devastation, however, comes a divine shaking, producing new blessing for our present that could never have been anticipated."*

People ask strange questions about the new heaven and the new earth. Will there be animals? Will we know each other? Will there be worship *and* work? The answer to all these questions is an absolute *yes!* The present earth is an imperfect but prophetic picture of what heaven will be like. The Scriptures declare that *all* things were created for God's pleasure (4:11). The animals were not created for *my* pleasure (although that is a side benefit), but for *His* pleasure. They give Him pleasure on the present earth that is passing away and will continue to bless His heart when all things become new.

He has created us for relationship with Himself *and* others. That is why our "neighbor" is so important in both Old and New Testaments. I am called to love God with all of my heart, soul, mind and strength, and my neighbor is to be loved with similar commitments (Matthew 26:39). All of this points to the rich relational connection we will have with one another in the Eternal Kingdom. Not only will we *know* our loved ones in heaven, but we will also know those that we *didn't* know on earth.

The three disciples recognized Moses and Elijah on the Mount of Transfiguration even though there was no possible way they could have known what these prophets looked like (Matthew 17:1-4). Doubtless this is included in what Paul is pointing to when he declares that for the present "we know in part" but "when perfection comes, the imperfect disappears" (1 Corinthians 13:9-10).

All of these Scriptures and perspectives speak of God's eternal plan for our future. This is why encountering Christ is so all-encompassing in the change that it brings: *He redeems my past, restores my present and promises glory for my future.*

In a loving relationship with God, there is no area of life that is left untouched, including my deepest pain and loss. When anyone is in "Christ, he is a new creation," the old has gone away and the new has come (2 Corinthians 5:17). It's a truly incredible promise that Christ will bring healing to my present *and* future. The reality of this promise, however, raises a significant question: If we experience a healing miracle in the present, what is the point of added new blessing in the future? Or another way of phrasing it is this: *Why will there be* tears *in heaven that Jesus needs to wipe away?* The answer lies in the nature of grief itself.

Immediately before and after the girls' funeral, our family walked in a confusing blur of pain. Certain things happened, however, that brought that blur into sharp focus for a moment in time. One of these moments happened for my wife on the evening of the funeral, several hours after the interment of our girls. We were in a home where dozens of people had gathered to bring food, comfort and support to our family. A woman my wife had not met until that moment (her name, we later learned, was Millie) quietly approached her, and in an intimate face-to-face moment shared that she and her husband had lost their 24-year-old son to cancer. Their loss had happened four years earlier, so these new friends were much further down the grief road than our family. She was able to assure Connie that Jesus would bring healing, and then she shared something that has helped us greatly during our healing journey.

At one point in the conversation, Millie gently touched my wife on the center of her chest close to her heart and quietly spoke these words, "You will learn to live with a sob that sits right here." Her words were both profound *and* prophetic for our family because they accurately describe our experience of healing to this present time.

I have attempted to outline in these chapters the deep healing and fruitfulness that are produced in our lives as we surrender to Christ in the *process* of grief and mourning. We must be absolutely adamant about this point: The Holy Spirit accomplishes extensive healing in our lives, and He has surely done so for me. I do *not* currently live my life in the grip of debilitating pain as I did in the early years, and I rejoice daily in the *new* blessings that have flooded my soul.

God's healing has been nothing short of miraculous, but I *still* live with a sob in my heart. There is a measure of pain that continues to mark me, and the ever-present sob can suddenly break forth at any moment. It's completely *unpredictable*.

Here's an example of what might incite the sob. I have a picture of René on my desk that was taken shortly before her death, and she is standing in the middle of a breathtaking rose garden. She is wearing a red blouse and black skirt, and her arms are outstretched as though to say, "Look at all of my beautiful flowers, Dad." It's one of my favorite pictures of her. Most days I look at that photograph with emotional control and thank God for the gift of her life. I picture her worshiping now in the presence of Jesus, and my heart is full of comfort and at rest. Occasionally, however, I look at the same picture and inexplicably the sob spills over. There is a portion of unhealed pain that will be with me *always* in this present life, and I have embraced the reality of this ubiquitous sob from a place of inner peace.

The good news in connection with this hidden sob, however, is that it's *not* the final chapter because the eternal hope of heaven awaits me. I will stand in the presence of my Lord and Savior on that final day, and the sob will break forth once more. Then, as Jesus *permanently* wipes away each tear from my eyes, the *substantial* healing will become *complete* healing, and I will be overcome with relentless, eternal joy. Then, too, the longing that I have for reunion with my loved ones will be forever satisfied.

*"The miracle of new blessing is both present and future, and to focus on either one at the exclusion of the other is to deprive us of God's full inheritance."*

The miracle of new blessing is both present and future, and to focus on either one at the exclusion of the other is to deprive us of God's full inheritance. As I embrace both parts simultaneously in faith, I am guaranteed present *and* future blessing, healing *and* fruitfulness.

## SUMMARY

**In the aftermath of catastrophic loss we must discover a new normal.** We can never make our lives the way they were before. Loss brings permanent, irrevocable and irreversible change. Any *prolonged* attempt to sustain my life the way it used to be will thwart healing, fruitfulness and new blessing, causing me to wander in a never-ending circle of anger, bitterness and denial.

**God's restoration will bring new blessing, healing and fruitfulness to my life.** Out of the rubble of pain, He builds something beautiful which releases His glory through me. The miraculous new blessing God brings will transcend what I knew in the past, establishing the certain promises of His great restoration Psalm: "Those who sow in tears will reap with songs of joy. He who goes out weeping, carrying seed to sow, will return with songs of joy, carrying sheaves with him" (126:5-6). There are no *wasted* tears in God's Kingdom. Each shed tear becomes precious seed that is planted in the soil of my pain, producing a great harvest of healing, restoration and new joy.

**To receive the new blessing, we must exercise our wills and open**

**our hearts in faith.** The gifts of God's grace are activated only when they are received *and* unwrapped. If my heart is hardened through anger turned to bitterness, a precious jewel of new blessing will be rejected and trampled upon. The solemn warning of Hebrews 4 rings true for our hearts today: ". . . The message they heard was of no value to them, because those who heard did not combine it with faith" (2). My tears *will* be turned to joy, but *only* as I embrace with open-hearted faith the new blessings and gifts that He brings.

**Complete healing and new fruitfulness are experienced in the acceptance of both present and future restoration, redemption and healing.** It's possible to miss the incredible gifts of God in the present by exclusively focusing on future promises.

Conversely, the present can never be fully enjoyed without seeing in faith our future and eternal hope. In the experience of loss and pain, it's possible to receive deep, extensive and substantial healing, but an ever-present sob continues to lodge in my heart. Complete healing will become reality in heaven when I encounter the Lamb "at the center of the throne." He will be my Shepherd, leading me to springs of living water, and He will wipe "away every tear" from my eyes (Revelation 7:17).

# CHAPTER 8

# The Person & the Promise

I would like to conclude the six principles set forth in this book by briefly considering the foundational cornerstone that supports them. This cornerstone is revealed in two ways—in a Person and through a promise.

*Our cornerstone, first of all, is found in a Person.* All the truth God desires to communicate finds its culmination and ultimate expression in Christ. The writer of Hebrews makes this crystal clear. God spoke to previous generations "at many times and in various ways, but in these last days He has spoken to us by His Son" (Hebrews 1:1). This Son is the "radiance of God's glory and the exact representation of His being," sustaining "all things by His powerful Word" (3).

Any truth encounter we will ever have is found and rooted in Christ. Whether we are looking for God's love, holiness, mercy, grace, power or justice, each is found in the *Person* of Christ. This is why Jesus can answer the question of the disciple Thomas with such an absolute truth claim: "'I am the Way and the Truth and the Life. No one comes to the Father except through Me'" (John 14:6).

We have spoken in previous chapters about the experience of healing and fruitfulness. Out of the rubble of personal pain and loss, God can create new blessings as we open our hearts to Him. This genuine restoration is experienced most completely in a personal relationship with Jesus. The principles of suffering loss and experiencing change, healing, restoration and fruitfulness draw their meaning, power and effectiveness from Christ Himself.

Jesus speaks in John 15 about the necessity of living in a close, dependent relationship with Him. As we abide or remain "in Him," fruitfulness is maximized. It's in the context of this teaching that He announces the following: "'I no longer call you servants, but instead have called you friends . . .'" (John 15:13-17). The placement of this statement is no accident because it's through personal friendship with Jesus that we experience healing. The Person of Christ *and* friendship with Him provide the cornerstone of support for the six principles discussed in our previous chapters.

*Our cornerstone not only is demonstrated in Christ's Person, but is secondly revealed through His promise.* There are numerous promises Jesus makes during His earthly ministry, but I focus on one that brings ultimate hope when we encounter death, loss and pain: "'I am the resurrection and the life. He who believes in Me will live, even though he dies; and whoever lives and believes in Me will never die'" (John 11:25-26). Our Lord makes this proclamation with authoritative certainty that is linked with what He is about to *do.* Jesus is poised to call Lazarus forth from the grave, giving an ultimate demonstration of His Lordship over death itself.

**"This reunion is not an illusion but an anchor, and it holds the ship of my life steady because of Christ's Person and promise."**

This resurrection declaration is quoted at most funerals and always on Easter Sunday because it's tremendously encouraging and straightforward in its meaning and application. The hope of the resurrection is found in His Person *and* promise, and the comfort this brings to someone suffering with grief and loss is deeply encouraging.

I never got to hold and embrace my granddaughter, Jessica Grace, in this life—but I will hold her in the Eternal Kingdom. And it has been 13 years (at the time of this writing) since I last touched the blonde hair of my beautiful firstborn, René. But a glorious reunion is coming—and I *will* see her soon. This is not some trite psychological compensation to maintain my sanity. This reunion is not an illusion but an anchor, and it holds the ship of my life steady because of Christ's Person and promise.

I would like to digress for a moment from the main thrust of this passage and consider the shortest verse in Holy Scriptures: "Jesus wept" (John 11:35). The One who has just made the proclamation of resurrection and life stands at the grave of Lazarus and weeps. I ask the obvious question debated by theologians for centuries: Why?

The preceding verses give us an important perspective on the tears of Jesus. When our Lord saw Mary and the Jews who had come along with her all weeping, we read, "He was deeply moved" (33). We cannot lightly gloss over this statement. He was *deeply* moved. The meaning of the Greek word is "to snort with anger" and "have indignation."

When Jesus saw the weeping of others, there was a deep stirring in His own spirit that produced a righteous anger, and I believe it was this anger that produced the tears. But we ask again, "Why is the Lord of Life weeping by a grave—and more significantly—why is He angry?"

In order to arrive at a final truth that will bring immense comfort to our hearts, let's look at some of the answers that have been set forth by others.

Some have suggested that Jesus wept because He loved Lazarus and had lost him. The deep friendship between Lazarus and Jesus is certainly well-documented in Scripture. In many ways, this family in Bethany provided the only home that Jesus knew during His earthly ministry. When word was sent to Jesus about the illness of Lazarus, it was referenced with the phrase, "'Lord, the one You *love* is sick'" (3, emphasis added). But what would be the point of crying at the tomb?

Jesus *knew* what He was going to do. The great miracle of this chapter was not ad-lib because Jesus stated that the sickness would not end in death, even though the revelation was given to Him that Lazarus had actually died (4, 12-13). Why would He shed tears over the death of a friend who would be embraced moments after His arrival on the scene?

It has also been asserted that Jesus wept because of the unbelief of the Jews (John 11:33). He had come to redeem the chosen people, and so many had rejected Him—but Jesus was well-acquainted with this unbelief. In the previous chapter, it had erupted into intense hostility where they had "picked up stones to stone Him" (10:31, 39). The hatred and unbelief of the Jews was not a *new* revelation to the Master, and John tells us that Jesus did not entrust Himself to the people—"for He knew all men" (2:24).

Some commentators have explained that our Lord's tears were produced by the unbelief of Martha and Mary. Because of close friendship, and all that He had invested in them, He expected a "higher" response. "I'm disappointed in you two because you should know better" is the essence of this interpretation. Both women did in effect say that He had failed them, throwing out the accusing phrase: "'If only You had been here'" our "'brother would not have died'" (11:22, 32). But Jesus uses the unbelief as an opportunity for teaching and further enlightenment, giving to Martha in a one-on-one conversation the glorious truth-promise about the resurrection.

Our Lord's tears are best understood in connection with the previously mentioned phrase, "deeply moved." The same words are repeated a second time, just before He commands the stone to be taken away (38). These tears, compressed between two declarations of indignation and anger, show us the deep emotions that were churning in our Lord's heart.

I believe the weeping of Jesus was rooted in pain because of what sin had brought into the world. He stood at a grave and confronted the evil fruits of sin (death itself) and was overcome with tears and righteous anger. He wept because there would come a day in *this* life when Lazarus would die again and loved ones would once more gather around his grave in grief. His tears were laced with anger because of what sin produces: Its wages are always death (Romans 6:23).

Jesus knew that each person is "destined to die," and that each individual death would bring devastating pain to those who were left behind. He was weeping at that moment for each person that would ever grieve over a loved one.

The Bible declares, "Jesus Christ is the same yesterday and today and forever" (Hebrews 13:8). This means that time itself is finite and created and that Jesus always lives in the eternal now. At the tomb of Lazarus, He wept for *my* pain in His eternal now. He saw the moment when I would stand by the casket of my girls as I cried out in the agony of my soul, "No one should have to bury his own child!" The tears of God Himself were shed for me as He saw me touching her long blonde hair for the last time.

My Lord stood in the town of Bethany in the year A.D. 30, and cried because He knew that the last enemy to be destroyed is death itself (1 Corinthians 15:26). He wept for my mom who fought for each breath in her final hours as her family stood helplessly by her side. He wept for my dad, who cried in deep frustration in the clutches of advanced Parkinson's disease, shaking so severely that he was unable to put two AA batteries into his disc player. He loved the Lord with all of his heart and was a powerful man, but was reduced to a broken physical shell in the last days of his life. At the tomb of Lazarus, Jesus wept for him, and for the son who sat by the bed as he took the final painful breath of this temporal life.

And to my friends who are reading this now, you have shed tears over lost loved ones. You may have wept bitterly as a marriage that you thought would last a lifetime came unraveled. You may be crying this day over a health problem or a difficulty that has caused you to feel alone and isolated. Maybe at this moment you feel shattered with emotional pain that has

*"Not only is the Lord with you, He has also wept for you."*

pierced your soul. Not only is the Lord with you, He has also wept for you. These tears are *not* tears of despair, somehow disconnected from His miraculous redemption, restoration and resurrection. They are tears of *identification*, God Himself feeling the depth of your pain as He weeps with you in His eternal now.

It's this incredible insight that David prophetically and poetically provided when he spoke of God's gathering up each tear, recording it in a book and lovingly placing each one in His bottle (Psalm 56:8). Our God is *never* detached from our pain and loss. He is eternally connected with us at the deepest emotional level.

This brings us full circle and back to our first principle in chapter two. We can *trust* the Lord. He loves us, hurts with us and, in a demonstration of powerful sovereignty, brings restoration to our pain and loss. For our final conclusion, I would like to offer a heartfelt prayer for each of my readers.

*Loving Father, I thank You for the deep healing that You bring into hurting lives. I pray at this moment that Your love will be made real to each reader. For those who may find themselves in the turbulent waters of pain, grief and loss, it is my prayer that the Person and comfort of the Holy Spirit will be released into each heart. We ask for grace to trust You with the questions that may never be answered on this side of eternity. Please help us to embrace the Cross, the process of mourning, and save us from false remedies that would short-circuit the deep healing that You desire to impart. For those who may feel overcome with anguish, I ask for Your presence to open a door of hope—hope for healing, hope for increased fruitfulness and hope for new blessing that will bring a restoration of joy and beauty into each life. In the natural, all these things are impossible, Lord, but we surrender now "to Him who is able to do immeasurably more than all we ask or imagine, according to His power that is at work within us, to Him be glory in the Church and in Christ Jesus throughout all generations, for ever and ever! Amen" (Ephesians 3:20-21).*

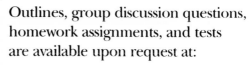